"A brilliant book! Brigham presents a compelling yet thoroughly practical vision of what the church could and should be in our times. Clarifying the church's mission as one of radical hospitality, Brigham brings personal experience, cutting edge philosophy, and nuanced theology into dialogue with actual church practices. This inspiring and well-written book will be accessible for undergraduates, thought-provoking for graduate students, and engaging for all who seek to follow Christ in the church today."

—Mary Doak, University of San Diego

Church as Field Hospital

Toward an Ecclesiology of Sanctuary

Erin Brigham

LITURGICAL PRESS
ACADEMIC

Collegeville, Minnesota
www.litpress.org

Library of Congress Cataloging-in-Publication Data

Names: Brigham, Erin, author.
Title: Church as field hospital : toward an ecclesiology of sanctuary / Erin Brigham.
Description: Collegeville, Minnesota : Liturgical Press Academic, [2022] | Includes index. | Summary: "Through an ethnographically-driven study of expressions of sanctuary in San Francisco, Church as Field Hospital constructs an ecclesiology that expands notions of public engagement and sacred space in Christian theology"— Provided by publisher.
Identifiers: LCCN 2021038886 (print) | LCCN 2021038887 (ebook) | ISBN 9780814667200 (paperback) | ISBN 9780814667217 (epub) | ISBN 9780814667217 (pdf)
Subjects: LCSH: Church. | BISAC: RELIGION / Christian Theology / Ecclesiology | RELIGION / Religion, Politics & State
Classification: LCC BV600.3 .B745 2022 (print) | LCC BV600.3 (ebook) | DDC 250—dc23
LC record available at https://lccn.loc.gov/2021038886
LC ebook record available at https://lccn.loc.gov/2021038887

Contents

Introduction

Context

"Are we not a sanctuary city?" a woman shouted into a microphone, evoking enthusiastic applause from the crowd of nearly three hundred people. Colorful banners and signs brought from congregations around the city adorned the walls of the parish hall of this Catholic church in San Francisco's Mission District. A group of pastors, priests, and rabbis in religious attire stood shoulder to shoulder as residents of the majority-Latinx neighborhood told their stories to city officials and demanded that they live up to the city's sanctuary commitment. Individual stories reinforced a common narrative—San Francisco is their home, and they are being pushed out because of the soaring cost of living. Although sanctuary was evoked, it was not primarily about the nation's exclusionary immigration policies—it was about housing and economic inequality. The speaker, a Latina in her sixties, talked about raising a family in San Francisco and the struggles she has experienced as her neighborhood has undergone rapid change in the past decade.

Faith in Action, a faith-based community organizing network, called the rally to push city officials to create more affordable housing. The recent construction of Casa Adelante, with 100 percent of the building's ninety units dedicated to affordable housing for seniors, seemed like a win for housing advocates. However, the rent was calculated by the income of residents in an area marked by rapid gentrification, amounting to over $3000 a month. UC Berkeley's Urban

1

Displacement Program found that the median income of the Mission District has changed significantly in the past two decades, rising from $46,749 in 1990 to $76,762 in 2013. This has coincided with a decrease of Latinx residents (44 percent–38 percent) and an increase in white residents (36 percent–43 percent).[1] Many San Franciscans like to celebrate our municipal sanctuary status as an expression of the city's progressive values. But today, sanctuary was evoked to resist another form of exclusion—a housing crisis pushing residents, particularly low-income people of color, out of the city or onto the streets.

Sanctuary is not commonly associated with inclusive housing in the way these activists have employed the concept. More frequently, sanctuary is associated with the convergence of faith-based and secular political movements that counter exclusionary immigration policies and enforcement methods. This book examines these expressions of sanctuary among other manifestations from a theological perspective, exploring sanctuary as *a way of being church*. To understand sanctuary from an ecclesiological perspective, I include sanctuary practices among immigrants as well as the unhoused. Studying churches that invite unhoused people to sleep in their worship space provides a context to explore the historical connection between sanctuary and sacred space, a connection that has been redefined by some contemporary expressions of sanctuary that emphasize public advocacy over spacesharing. Practices of sanctuary among the unhoused not only reveal the interconnectedness of inequality, homelessness, and exclusionary immigration policies, they embody a particular theology that has practical implications on what it means to declare and enact sanctuary.

Today, more than seventy US cities and eleven states have declared sanctuary, characterized by a refusal to employ local police to enforce

---

1. Sydney Cespedes, Mitchell Crispell, Christina Blackston, Jonathan Plowman, and Edward Graves, "Community Organizing and Resistance in SF's Mission District: Case Study on Gentrification and Displacement Pressures in the Mission District of San Francisco, CA," Center for Community Innovation, University of California, Berkeley (June 2015), at https://www.urbandisplacement.org/case-studies/ucb#section-46, accessed on July 23, 2020.

federal immigration policy.[2] Actual policies and practices between sanctuary cities vary, but the most basic idea is that when an immigrant is detained by the police, they will not automatically be held by a detainer, a request from the US Department of Immigration and Customs Enforcement (ICE) to hold the person for the purposes of immigration enforcement. From a legal perspective, the primary rationale behind sanctuary is pragmatic, according to Bill Ong Hing, an expert in immigration law and sanctuary policies. Sanctuary policies promote public safety by encouraging entire communities, regardless of immigration status, to trust local police.[3] Beyond legal and pragmatic arguments, sanctuary is often motivated by explicit values of inclusion, diversity, equity, hospitality, solidarity, and social justice. Yet, as ethicist Gary Slater has pointed out, the baseline definition of a sanctuary city as a space of noncooperation with federal immigration enforcement is ethically open-ended. It does not guarantee safety of migrants or the conditions for their flourishing. As the San Francisco housing activists illustrate concretely, Slater points out, "many sanctuary cities can in fact be stratified, unequal, and isolated spaces, with little accommodation for their undocumented populations beyond tolerance of their basic physical presence."[4]

In the United States today, over one thousand faith communities, sometimes in tandem with local ordinances, have declared sanctuary. As is the case with municipal sanctuary, these declarations have various meanings but coalesce around the commitment to "protect and stand

---

2. The nonpartisan think tank Center for Immigration Studies, which favors "less immigration" but considers itself "pro-immigrant," publishes a list of sanctuary cities, counties, and states at https://cis.org/Map-Sanctuary-Cities-Counties-and-States (updated August 2020).

3. Bill O. Hing, "Immigration Sanctuary Policies: Constitutional and Representative of Good Policing and Good Public Policy," *UC Irvine Law Review* 2 (2012): 247–311, at 249. Hing outlines the constitutionality of sanctuary cities by emphasizing the public safety rationale as a legitimate expression of local autonomy from federal interference.

4. Gary Slater, "From Strangers to Neighbors: Toward an Ethics of Sanctuary Cities," *Journal of Moral Theology* 7, no. 2 (2018): 57–85, at 60.

with immigrants facing deportation."[5] The Oakland-based Interfaith Movement for Human Integrity describes four features of faith-driven sanctuary today: advocacy, accompaniment, freedom campaigns, and congregational housing.[6]

In my research with Catholic and Protestant sanctuary congregations in San Francisco, I found the practice of congregational housing to be a less common feature of sanctuary in comparison to the practices of public advocacy and accompaniment. At first glance, it seems like sanctuary has lost its historical connection to space. Yet there are approaches to sanctuary that emphasize space-sharing, challenging a neoliberal approach to private property that dominates cities like San Francisco.[7] In addition to the aforementioned housing activists appealing to San Francisco's sanctuary identity, there are congregations in San Francisco who practice "urban sanctuary," inviting unhoused neighbors to sleep in the worship space. This approach to sanctuary among the unhoused does not replace sanctuary among immigrants. Sanctuary as advocacy, accompaniment, and resistance to unjust deportations and detention of migrants represents an urgent task for religious and secular entities. However, when sanctuary is considered within the framework of Christian theology, there is a radical call to solidarity with the marginalized that involves an ethical discernment around private property.

This book explores sanctuary as a way of being church, informed by concrete ecclesial practices in conversation with historical and con-

---

5. Sanctuary coalitions across the United States have partnered to create a repository of resources and map of sanctuary congregations at https://www.sanctuarynotdeportation .org/.

6. Interfaith Movement for Human Integrity at https://www.im4humanintegrity .org/.

7. I am using the term neoliberalism to refer to policies that favor the free market over governmental intervention. Features of neoliberalism include deregulation of national and international environmental and labor standards and reduction in welfare programs. These policies are informed by and reinforce a view of the person as autonomous and self-interested. For perspectives on neoliberalism, see *Social Justice and Neoliberalism: Global Perspectives*, ed. Adrian Smith, Alison Stenning, and Katie Willis (London: Zed Books, 2008).

structive ecclesiologies. Specifically, I present sanctuary as a tangible expression of Pope Francis's emerging ecclesiology that envisions the church as a field hospital. This ecclesiology connects the prophetic witness of the church with embodied practices of solidarity. A field hospital is porous and mobile to meet people where they are. Yet a field hospital functions as a space set apart: a physical space for the most vulnerable. Although Francis does not evoke the word sanctuary, his social teaching insists that we must not only denounce structural exclusion but that the church must be a space—metaphorically and literally—where those who have been excluded find a home. The pope has welcomed refugee families to stay at the Vatican and challenged all churches of Europe to follow his example. He also transformed Vatican property into a home for the unhoused. Through these practices, Francis challenges the church to embody solidarity with the marginalized, to go out to the peripheries of society and allow the oppressed to transform the church into a "poor church for the poor."

Solidarity with the marginalized is at the heart of espoused theologies of sanctuary. Congregations promise to accompany migrants vulnerable to deportation and to stand with them through public witness and advocacy against what they perceive to be unjust immigration policies. The context of San Francisco is, in many ways, helpful toward building solidarity through sanctuary. It is a sanctuary city with progressive immigration courts,[8] multicultural communities, and a history of activism. On the other hand, it is increasingly difficult for the nonwealthy to live in the city. The economic inequality that characterizes California, in general, is concentrated in this urban center.[9]

---

8. TRAC, a nonpartisan, nonprofit data research center at Syracuse University, compares denial rates of asylum cases across cities. Based on data between 2014–2019, San Francisco has a 30 percent denial rate, while Houston judges, on average, deny 92 percent of asylum cases. TRAC, "Asylum Denial Rates by Immigration Court and Judge" available at https://trac.syr.edu/immigration/reports/590, accessed on Oct. 14, 2020.

9. Statewide the disparity between the top 10 percent and bottom 10 percent of earners was $262,000 versus $21,000 respectively in 2018. The Bay Area represents the greatest regional disparity in California ($384,000 versus $32,000). Public Policy Institute of California (January 2020), at https://www.ppic.org/publication/income -inequality-in-california/.

Despite tenants' rights such as rent control, the housing market shifts to favor the wealthy. Despite the history of antiestablishment, slow-growth activism, many argue the city has catered to the interests of large corporations, pointing to the 2011 Twitter tax exemption as evidence.[10]

In this context, the most prophetic practices of sanctuary are those that resist the logic of neoliberalism—demonstrating the limitations of private property by sharing space with the person left vulnerable by an unjust economy, criminal justice system, and immigration policies. These disruptive practices of sanctuary go beyond the pragmatic approach of noninterference, offering a more robust vision of the common good that celebrates human interdependence. Throughout history, sanctuary has been constructed by a combination of ethical and pragmatic, religious and political, motivations. A brief overview of the research presents sanctuary as a negotiation of space and power based on cultural and religious assumptions about sacred space and the relationship between the church and politics.

Understanding Sanctuary

Much of the research on sanctuary has been by historians and anthropologists, who have demonstrated that some form of sanctuary exists in most religions and cultures.[11] Linda Rabben argues that sanctuary is a basic expression of "reciprocal altruism," shared not only across cultures but also with some primates.[12] In complex societies, sanctuary exists within tensions around inclusion and exclusion—who is defined as other and who is offered refuge—within cultural, economic, and po-

---

10. In 2011 the San Francisco Board of Supervisors passed the Mid-Market/Tenderloin Tax Incentive, which exempted companies moving into the mid-market area from payroll tax for new employees for six years. The connection between such policies and economic exclusion will be made in chapter 1.

11. Linda Rabben, *Sanctuary and Asylum: A Social and Political History* (Seattle: University of Washington Press, 2016); Philip Marfleet, "Understanding 'Sanctuary': Faith and Traditions of Asylum," *Journal of Refugee Studies* 24, no. 3 (September 2011): 440–55.

12. Rabben, *Sanctuary and Asylum*, 29.

litical structures that change over time. Several scholars have examined historical practices of sanctuary in order to understand and, in some cases, defend its contemporary expressions.[13]

Because the roots of sanctuary in the Hebrew Bible and early Christian practices have been particularly influential on contemporary religious and secular expressions of sanctuary in Europe and North America, I focus on this trajectory.[14] The Hebrew Bible identifies six cities of refuge, where an innocent person convicted of murder can seek refuge and avoid the penalty of death (Num 35:15). Scholars have noted the significance of this practice within the context of a blood vengeance system, wherein family members were obligated to avenge the death of kin by killing the aggressor. The practice of asylum or refuge among the Israelites and other ancient Near East cultures preserved this social practice by distinguishing between intentional and unintentional killing.[15] Cities of refuge were not only set aside to protect innocent Israelites but also the "resident alien," who is the subject of several biblical texts mandating mercy toward the stranger.[16]

Central to the practice of sanctuary was the designation of the sacred as something set apart. All cities of refuge identified in the Bible are Levite cities, highlighting the significance of the priest in signifying the holiness of the space. The person seeking refuge had to remain in the city until the death of the high priest, suggesting a theology of atonement connected to the practice.[17] An earlier and less developed practice of sanctuary in the Hebrew Bible was connected specifically to the holy space of the altar. The book of Exodus describes a person

13. Ignatius Bau, *This Ground Is Holy: Church Sanctuary and Central American Refugees* (Mahwah, NJ: Paulist Press, 1985); William Ryan, "The Historical Case for the Right of Sanctuary," *Journal of Church and State* 29, no. 2 (Spring 1987): 209–32; Rabben, *Sanctuary and Asylum.*

14. Bau, *This Ground Is Holy.*

15. David Ewert, "Avenger of Blood," in *The Oxford Companion to the Bible* (Oxford: Oxford University Press, 1993).

16. Chad Thomas Beck, "Sanctuary for Immigrants and Refugees in Our Legal and Ethical Wilderness," *Interpretation: A Journal of Bible and Theology* 72, no. 2 (2018): 132–45.

17. Bau, *This Ground Is Holy*, 125–26.

fleeing vengeance running to the altar to avoid retribution.[18] In his historical overview of sanctuary, Ignatius Bau argues that these two types of biblical sanctuary—one delineated by the holiness of the altar and the communitarian form associated with a city of refuge—are both influential in subsequent developments of sanctuary in the Jewish and Christian traditions.[19]

The earliest documented practices of sanctuary in the Christian tradition are laid out in the Theodosian Code of 392 CE, after Christianity gained favor in the Roman Empire under Constantine's authority. Initially, the interior space of the church was to be a place of refuge for certain people accused of crimes. Christian sanctuary, from its onset, relied on assumptions about who was eligible and who was to be excluded.[20] People were excluded based on the nature of the crime, with debtors and embezzlers exempt from sanctuary. People were also excluded based on their relationship to the church, with Jews, heretics, and apostates considered ineligible for sanctuary. The power to exclude is one of the ways sanctuary became a tool to elevate the authority of the church, specifically of the bishop. Sanctuary developed during this period and in 450 CE, the exterior courtyard of the church as well as the bishop's house were considered spaces of refuge. Sanctuary further advanced the authority of the church by reinforcing the delineation of sacred from the profane. Bau argues that keeping sanctuary-seekers in the courtyard of the church, near the holy but without access to the holiest of places, reinforced the power of sacred space.[21]

Focusing on the tension between sacred and profane, Bau traces the development of sanctuary from early Christian practices to the highly institutionalized medieval practice as a move away from the authority of the church space to the authority of the bishop. The power of the bishop was reinforced by Pope Leo I (440–61 CE), who decreed

18. Jonathan Burnside, "Exodus and Asylum: Uncovering the Relationship between Biblical Law and Narrative," *Journal for the Study of the Old Testament* 34, no. 3 (Mar 2010): 243–66.

19. Bau, *This Ground Is Holy*.

20. Bau, *This Ground Is Holy*, 131; and Rabben, *Sanctuary and Asylum*, 39–42.

21. Bau, *This Ground Is Holy*, 131.

that church authorities must review sanctuary cases.[22] The medieval practices of sanctuary in particular highlight the dynamic negotiation of ecclesial and political authority. The power of sanctuary relied on the holiness of church space and reinforced the authority of the church hierarchy. While this served the political interests of the king by maintaining peace and order, it also elevated the church, a competing authority.

Gradually, church sanctuary was placed under juridical authority of the kings of England, with several restrictions that consolidated their secular authority, while leveraging the authority of the church. English king Ethelbert of Kent used his authority to establish strict punishment for those who violated the peace of the church or *fryth* in 597 CE.[23] During this period, a number of churches, abbeys, and cloisters were elevated as sanctuaries, making sanctuary more widespread and political. Abuses of sanctuary abounded as these spaces were sought increasingly by people fleeing from debt collectors.[24] When monarchies added restrictions on sanctuary, the Catholic Church pushed back with the threat of excommunication.[25]

Although sanctuary was officially abolished by English law in 1624 and eliminated in canon law in 1983,[26] it persisted because of its cultural power. Modern expressions of sanctuary in North America rely on cultural and religious sensibility more than legal authority. Sanctuary was first evoked in North America to defend conscientious objectors to the Vietnam War.[27] Protestant Minister William Sloane Coffin Jr. drew an explicit connection to church sanctuary in the past to argue for

22. Bau, *This Ground Is Holy*, 131; and Rabben, *Sanctuary and Asylum*, 40.

23. Ryan, "The Historical Case for the Right of Sanctuary," 217.

24. Bau, *This Ground Is Holy*, 150.

25. Hilary Cunningham, *God and Caesar at the Rio Grande: Sanctuary and the Politics of Religion* (Minneapolis: University of Minnesota Press, 1995), 81.

26. Cunningham, *God and Caesar,* 81–82.

27. Cunningham, *God and Caesar.* While the language of sanctuary to describe civil disobedience in North America was first evoked in this context, it is important to highlight how the Underground Railroad provided sanctuary and protection to African Americans fleeing slavery in the South. Later expressions of sanctuary would evoke the Underground Railroad to describe and legitimate their own civil disobedience.

sanctuary for conscientious objectors in 1966: "Now if in the Middle Ages churches could offer sanctuary to the most common of criminals, could they not today do the same for the most conscientious among us?"[28] Churches became public sanctuaries for people resisting the draft; however, this did not stop police and military authorities from entering churches and prosecuting conscientious objectors seeking refuge.[29]

The most prominent sanctuary movement in North America was in response to the large number of Salvadoran and Guatemalan asylum seekers who fled to the United States during their country's civil wars.[30] Central American asylum seekers were routinely denied asylum, with the Reagan administration arguing that they migrated for economic reasons, not human rights violations.[31] Faith communities organized to protect, defend, and advocate for the rights of migrants under the banner of sanctuary. Sanctuary practices varied according to location, with the primary sanctuary coalitions emerging on the US-Mexico border, especially Tucson, as well as Chicago and the San Francisco Bay Area.

Tucson-based sanctuary emerged as a humanitarian response to migrants making the dangerous border-crossing in the Sonoran Desert. Jim Corbett, a Quaker rancher, and John Fife, a Presbyterian minister, began organizing a network of sanctuary volunteers who guided asylum seekers across the border to take refuge in their churches and homes. Fife compared this work to the protection of refugees in Nazi Germany and the protection of slaves through the Underground Railroad. Sanctuary in this context was perceived as a faith-driven response

---

28. Rev. William Coffrey Sloane, Jr., quoted in Barbara L. Bezdek, "Religious Outlaws: Narratives of Legality and the Politics of Citizen Interpretation," *Tennessee Law Review* 62 (1995): 899–996, at 934.

29. Bezdek, "Religious Outlaws."

30. Between 1979 and 1986, over one million Central Americans entered the United States (Edelberto Torres-Rivera, Report on the Condition of Central American Refugees and Migrants [Washington, DC: Center for Immigration and Refugee Assistance, Georgetown University, July 1985]. Quoted in Hilary Cunningham, "Sanctuary and Sovereignty: Church and State Along the US-Mexico Border," *Journal of Church and State* 40, no. 2 (Spring 1998): 371–86, at 374.

31. Cunningham, "Sanctuary and Sovereignty," 375.

to a higher moral law, which in this case opposed state law. Fife, quoting Corbett, writes, "We can serve the Kingdom, or we can serve the kingdoms of this world—but we cannot do both."[32]

Alison Cunningham's research on Tucson-based sanctuary examines sanctuary as a dynamic negotiation of church and state power. Sanctuary workers in this context articulated their practices in terms of acts of conscience, practicing Christianity in this case entailed defying unjust laws. The federal government asserted its authority over sanctuary volunteers through Operation Sojourner, an FBI and INS operation in 1983 which involved an investigation of Southside Presbyterian Church in Tucson. As a result of Operation Sojourner, sixteen sanctuary volunteers were indicted by a federal court, facing numerous charges related to "harboring and transporting illegal aliens."[33] During the sanctuary trial, the defense evoked the First Amendment, defending the autonomy of the church from state oversight and the church's right to practice sanctuary as an expression of their faith.[34] This case revealed how sanctuary both defied the privatization of religion by connecting faith to political activism but also how it relied on a nonlegally binding cultural sensibility that regarded sacred spaces as something set apart.

As the sanctuary movement grew in Arizona, shaped particularly by its proximity to the US-Mexico border, sanctuary coalitions emerged in Chicago and the San Francisco Bay Area. Robin Lorentzen points to different approaches in Tucson and Chicago, claiming that Tucson was focused on immediate humanitarian service, while Chicago was building a national political network. The Chicago sanctuary coalition emphasized public advocacy through public witness and civil disobedience. Chicago-based sanctuary was led primarily by women,

---

32. Jim Corbett, quoted in John Fife, "From the Sanctuary Movement to No More Deaths: The Challenge to Communities of Faith," in *Religious and Ethical Perspectives on Global Migration*, ed. Charles Strain (Landham: Lexington, 2014), 259.

33. Kristina Campbell, "Operation Sojourner: The Government Infiltration of the Sanctuary Movement in the 1980s and Its Legacy on the Modern Central American Refugee Crisis," *University of St. Thomas Law Journal* 13, no. 3 (2016): 474–507.

34. Cunningham, *God and Caesar*.

particularly Catholic sisters, which Lorentzen regards as significant. Despite the media attention given to male sanctuary leaders, particularly Corbett and Fife, Lorentzen claims that women had a central role in the "caretaking" work of sanctuary. This included humanitarian caretaking—hosting asylum seekers and providing accompaniment, as well as political caretaking—forging the network of volunteers and coordinating public witness.[35] Emphasizing public advocacy, some of the Chicago sanctuary workers were critical of "paternalistic" sanctuary practices that focused on direct service and protection of migrants. Lorentzen analyzes this through the lens of gender, noting that the women leaders, particularly Catholic sisters, interpreted the theologically mandated preferential option for the poor and oppressed to include liberation of women.[36]

Sanctuary emerged in the Bay Area around six congregations reading Scripture together in light of liberation theology and violence against church leaders in El Salvador. The killing of archbishop Oscar Romero in 1980 became a focal point for understanding transnational solidarity among these churches. Focusing on this context, anthropologist Susan Bibler Coutin understands sanctuary primarily as a form of religious civil disobedience. Coutin argues that the religious narratives such as welcoming the stranger, along with public prayer rituals, reinforced the moral authority, justice orientation, and interfaith dimension of sanctuary.[37] Migrant testimony was incorporated into public witness and religious services with a dual purpose of consciousness-raising and conversion toward the poor. The themes of liberation theology, particularly solidarity with the poor and marginalized, were at the center of Christian sanctuary. This theology, which emphasized orthopraxis (right action) over orthodoxy (right

35. Robin Lorentzen, *Women in the Sanctuary Movement* (Philadelphia: Temple University Press, 1991).

36. The way the Catholic sisters framed the feminist goals of liberation theology, however, did not always resonate with the migrants they sought to empower (Lorentzen, *Women in the Sanctuary Movement*).

37. Susan Bibler Coutin, *The Culture of Protest: Religious Activism and the U.S. Sanctuary Movement* (Boulder: Westview Press, 1993), chapter 10.

teaching) fueled religious activism and transnational solidarity with the poor. Coutin argues that solidarity was a driving principle of the sanctuary movement but that the emphasis on religious conversion which relied on a "quasi-sacred status" of migrants reinforced their "otherness" among mostly white, upper-middle-class North Americans. She notes that sanctuary participants themselves were critical of paternalistic and potentially exploitative dimensions of sanctuary as they sought to build transnational solidarity.[38]

In the Bay Area, nineteen congregations had declared sanctuary by 1989. Many of them followed a process of discernment that involved learning about the realities of asylum seekers and the impact of US foreign policy toward Central America in conversation with theological and ethical reflection.[39] Practically speaking, by declaring sanctuary, congregations promised to protect, defend, and advocate for migrants. Faith communities provided an ethical framework for city officials to consider sanctuary as a municipal ordinance.[40] San Francisco officially became a sanctuary city in 1985, joining other municipalities in the refusal to leverage local law enforcement in federal immigration enforcement measures. Municipal and congregational sanctuary raised consciousness about the injustices in the Central American civil wars and of the United States' relationship to El Salvador. This intensified around the 1989 murder of six Jesuits, along with their housekeeper and her daughter at the University of Central America by a US-trained soldier.[41] This reexamination of US foreign policy resulted in the Immigration Act of 1990, which created Temporary Protected Status

---

38. Coutin, *Culture of Protest*, 183–87.

39. Peter Mancina, "The Birth of a Sanctuary-City: A History of Governmental Sanctuary in San Francisco," in *Sanctuary Practices in International Perspectives: Migration, Citizenship, and Social Movements*, ed. Randy Lippert and Sean Rehagg (London: Routledge, 2013), 209.

40. Mancina, "The Birth of a Sanctuary-City."

41. Hector Perla Jr. and Susan Bibler Coutin, "Legacies and Origins of the 1980s US–Central American Sanctuary Movement," in Lippert and Rehagg, *Sanctuary Practices*, 73–91, at 82.

(TPS) for certain groups whose homeland is unsafe due to conflict, natural disaster, or other extraordinary conditions.[42]

TPS did not end deportations of Central American migrants fearful of returning home because of widespread violence. Deportations increased significantly from 2000–2010.[43] These have been the focus of the New Sanctuary Movement. The New Sanctuary Movement launched in 2007 in response to increased deportations and attempts to pass the Sensenbrenner Bill (2005) that would make assisting undocumented migrants a felony act. High profile sanctuary cases focused on migrants taking refuge in churches to avoid deportation, which often meant family separation. These include Elvira Arellano, who took refuge in a Chicago church in 2006, and Jeanette Vizguerra, who similarly sought refuge in a Denver church. Although these cases increased the visibility of sanctuary, church spaces are not off-limits for ICE activity any more than schools, hospitals, or courthouses. In a 2011 memo, ICE described its policy of restraining from surveillance or enforcement in these "sensitive areas," but this practice is not codified in law.[44]

Physical sanctuary is one of the less common dimensions of the New Sanctuary Movement. In her ethnographic study of sanctuary as a multifaceted social movement, Grace Yukich notes that sanctuary is a moniker within a host of interfaith strategies to stop deportations and promote just immigration policy.[45] The New Sanctuary Movement gained more visibility after the inauguration of President Donald

42. Perla and Coutin, "The US-Central American Sanctuary Movement."

43. The Pew Research Center reports 188,000 removals in 2000 and 395,000 in 2009. See the Pew Research Center, "As Deportations Rise to Record Levels, Most Latinos Oppose Obama's Policy," December 2011, at https://www.pewresearch.org/hispanic/2011/12/28/as-deportations-rise-to-record-levels-most-latinos-oppose-obamas-policy/.

44. John Morton, Memorandum to Field Office Directors, Special Agents in Charge, and Chief Counsel, "Enforcement Actions at or Focused on Sensitive Locations," October 24, 2011, at https://www.ice.gov/doclib/ero-outreach/pdf/10029.2-policy.pdf.

45. Grace Yukich, *One Family under God: Immigration Politics and Progressive Religion in America* (Oxford: Oxford University Press, 2013).

Trump in 2017. Trump, who ran on an anti-immigration platform, immediately began issuing executive orders aimed to strengthen border security and curb migration from Muslim-majority countries.[46] Churches and synagogues began issuing public declarations of sanctuary while sanctuary cities also grew in number. Yukich observes dual aims in faith-based sanctuary practice today. In addition to the goal of justice for immigrants, sanctuary serves as a way for religious congregations to reform and assert their religious identities as interfaith and progressive.[47]

Recent studies of sanctuary cities have included analyses of power and have offered critical approaches to sanctuary. Randy Lippert and Peter Mancina analyze how sanctuary cities represent a different form of governmentality that challenges notions of citizenship (Mancina) and compensates for the declining welfare state under advanced liberalism (Lippert).[48] Focusing on sanctuary practices in Canada, Lippert points to sanctuary "instances" as opposed to a cohesive movement. Jennifer Ridgley has examined sanctuary not only from the perspective of state power but through abolitionist-oriented grassroots movements that challenge the criminalization of migration and power of the state to arrest, detain, and deport.[49] Ridgley, along with Naomi Paik, is critical

---

46. See executive orders "Border Security and Immigration Enforcement Improvements," "Enhancing Public Safety in the Interior of the United States," and "Protecting the Nation from Foreign Terrorist Entry into the United States," issued on January 25 and March 6, 2017 (Exec. Order 13,767; Exec. Order 13,768; and Exec. Order 13,780). For a critical analysis, see Naomi Paik, "Abolitionist Futures and the US Sanctuary Movement," *Race and Class* 59, no. 2 (2017): 3–25.

47. Yukich, *One Family under God.*

48. Randy K. Lippert, *Sanctuary, Sovereignty, Sacrifice: Canadian Sanctuary Incidents, Power, and Law* (Vancouver: University of British Columbia Press, 2005); and Peter Mancina, *In the Spirit of Sanctuary: Sanctuary-City Policy Advocacy and the Production of Sanctuary-Power in San Francisco, California* (PhD diss., Vanderbilt University, 2016).

49. Jennifer Ridgley, *Cities of Refuge: Citizenship, Legality, and Exception in U.S. Sanctuary Cities* (PhD diss., University of Toronto, 2010). See also Fiona Jeffries and Jennifer Ridgley, "Building the Sanctuary City from the Ground Up: Abolitionist Solidarity and Transformative Reform," *Citizenship Studies* 24, no. 4 (2020): 548–67.

of rhetoric that reinforces the ideal immigrant within a familial and capitalist framework; that is, the hardworking person providing for their family. They advocate for a more radical form of sanctuary that disrupts the pattern of racialized criminalization and profit-driven mass incarceration.[50] This critique is particularly relevant in the United States, but by focusing on sanctuary practices in Canada (Ridgley and Lippert) and the United Kingdom and Europe (Rabben), scholars demonstrate that sanctuary exists beyond its particular form in US politics.[51]

This brief historical overview, by no means exhaustive, is meant to illustrate the diverse expressions of sanctuary, while also situating this particular study of sanctuary, which is shaped by Christian theology and practice, in San Francisco. Throughout history, sanctuary has involved a negotiation of space around ecclesiological questions. Concretely, practices of sanctuary have been shaped by theological understandings of sacred space, as well as how sacred space is distinguished from nonsacred space. Practicing sanctuary therefore reinforces ecclesial borders while simultaneously opening those boundaries for some, though not all, people. Most research on sanctuary, faith-based and secular, comes from anthropology and political science. This book focuses on the ecclesiology of sanctuary—how it expresses and gives rise to a particular way of being church. It goes beyond examining sanctuary from the perspective of church-state relations to ask—what is the theological understanding of the church in the context of sanctuary?

Research Questions

An Ecclesiological Focus

My interest in sanctuary began in 2017, when my church made a public declaration of our commitment to accompany and advocate for immigrants. I began attending know your rights trainings in the worship space, listening to stories of our undocumented neighbors living in

---

50. Paik, "Abolitionist Futures."
51. Lippert, *Sanctuary and Sovereignty*.

fear of deportation, and joining an interfaith coalition of sanctuary congregations in resistance. I found myself paying attention to the ways in which faith was being practiced and articulated in public spaces, wanting to better understand the theology behind these expressions of church. Originally thinking of this as an interview-based project only, I met with a community organizer with Faith in Action and asked her to help me set up the research project on the ecclesiology of sanctuary. She helped me identify leading voices across Catholic and Protestant churches who had declared sanctuary, were discerning sanctuary, or practicing sanctuary. I wanted to better understand the ecclesiologies of sanctuary, both implicit and articulated, from people who identified sanctuary as an expression of the Christian faith. As an organizer, she wanted to promote more widespread commitment and engagement among sanctuary churches.

I originally set up this research project to pursue theological knowledge together with communities who identify in some way with sanctuary, in order to deepen our understanding of how a community's ecclesiology (theological understanding of church) informs and is informed by their approach to sanctuary. This study focuses on practices of sanctuary, the process of discernment around sanctuary, and the public declaration of sanctuary. Specifically, I initially pursued the following questions: What are the implicit ecclesiologies behind concrete expressions of sanctuary? Are there unifying principles, narratives, and themes that transcend denominations, political leanings, and theological self-understandings? How does a community arrive at a commitment to sanctuary? Does this process of discernment reveal shifts in the self-understanding of the church? How do these self-understandings relate to ecclesial practice? How do other social, cultural, and economic factors intersect with ecclesial identity and public engagement?

The significance of this project extends beyond the practice of sanctuary. It contributes to larger ecclesiological questions related to the relationship between the church and modern society and the way the church engages the public sphere and exercises political resistance. Observing how different churches exercise sanctuary invites an examination of how theological concepts like sanctuary are translated into public discourse and practices. Exploring how communities practice, discern, and declare sanctuary provides a context to understand the ways theology becomes public and how communities with less power in relation to the dominant public sphere create alternative public spaces. It has also pointed to the limits of translation, shaped by a narrow understanding of public reason.[52] The sanctuary practices I observed rely on narrative, performance, and testimony to articulate an ethical-theological resistance to unjust immigration policies.

My abiding research questions have been ecclesiological, but the contour of the questions have shifted. After two years and over twenty interviews with sanctuary practitioners, I have found myself volunteering biweekly at a church whose doors are opened each morning so unhoused people can sleep in the pews. This practice of sanctuary has allowed me to reflect on the significance of space, a question that kept emerging for me as I talked to people whose sanctuary commitment does not revolve around space-sharing. In this seven-by-seven-mile sanctuary city, the average cost of renting a one-bedroom apartment exceeds $3,000 a month.[53] The housing crisis, high cost of living, and radical income inequality makes private property a powerful resource and a site of moral discernment. As I became more involved in advocacy for unhoused San Franciscans, the interconnections of poverty, race, and nationality became more evident.

One of the churches in the study provided physical sanctuary for an asylum-seeking family from Mexico. Faith in Action connected the mother to the church after learning that the family had slept on the streets after losing their place at a temporary shelter. It was their experience of homelessness, interconnected to their experience as migrants,

---

52. I am using public reason in a Rawlsian sense, which suggests all norms and laws governing public life should be justified through generally accessible claims that appeal to reason rather than religious doctrine. This will be developed in chapter 2.

53. This reflects the average rent at the time I started this project (2017). The average rent of a one-bedroom apartment in San Francisco dropped 23.2 percent during the COVID-19 pandemic but is beginning to increase again to $2,082 as I conclude this project in March 2021. San Francisco rent report provided by Apartment List (April 2021), available at https://www.apartmentlist.com/ca/san-francisco#rent-report.

that challenged the church to become a sanctuary. There is nothing about San Francisco's legal sanctuary ordinance that would prompt this faith community to reexamine the radically unequal distribution of private property and housing crisis in this city. However, sanctuary informed by a faith that proclaims a preferential option for the poor and oppressed challenges the neoliberal assumptions behind oppressive inequity.

My attention has moved from a curiosity about how the church enters into the public sphere, especially in a secular context like San Francisco, toward questions revolving around the nature of sacred space itself and how sacred space gives rise to and is shaped by sanctuary practices. These questions are interdependent, I argue, because the way faith communities exercise public impact is through embodying their theologies through concrete spatial practices. As I volunteered among people experiencing homelessness and participated in sanctuary advocacy through my church, I observed how those who had been marginalized exercised their agency as cocreators of sanctuary. Immigrants disrupt narratives of exclusion through public testimony. Unhoused people delineate a personal space in the church through rituals associated with home. From this point of view, sanctuary is not so much something that the church possesses and offers; rather, sanctuary emerges when the church cocreates an alternative space to contest displacement and marginalization.

Theology and Ethnography

Because my research questions revolved around the theology embedded and generated in concrete practices, I turned to ethnographically driven methods. I joined a growing community of scholars integrating ethnography and theology, particularly practical theology and ecclesiology.[54] Behind this methodological shift is the assumption that

54. See *Explorations in Ecclesiology and Ethnography*, ed. Christian B. Scharen (Grand Rapids: Eerdmans, 2012); *Ethnography as Christian Theology and Ethics*, ed. Aana Marie Vigen and Christian B. Scharen (London: Continuum, 2011); *Perspectives on Ecclesiology and Ethnography*, ed. Pete Ward (Grand Rapids: Eerdmans, 2012). See also *Ecclesial Practices: Journal of Ecclesiology and Ethnography* (Brill).

ecclesiology cannot be reduced to a systematic or objective pursuit and that qualitative methods are viable tools not only for pastoral theology but for constructive and formal theologies as well.[55]

Articulating a methodology that combines practical theology and action research, Helen Cameron, Deborah Bhatti, Catherine Duce, James Sweeney, and Clare Watkins assert, "Practices of faithful Christian people are themselves already the bearers of theology; they express the contemporary living tradition of the Christian faith."[56] This project has been guided by a number of theoretical commitments laid out in Theological Action Research (TAR).[57] Specifically, I approached the communities engaged in sanctuary with the conviction that theology is disclosed in concrete sanctuary practices. I sought to discover how diverse sanctuary practices and recurring theological themes were not only expressing the implicit ecclesiology of the practicing community but could also be brought into a mutually transformative conversation with formal ecclesiology, particularly the thought of Pope Francis. From the onset, my interest has been not only to understand the ecclesiology of sanctuary but to articulate it in such a way that reinforces ecclesial practice and deepens congregational participation.

Cameron et al. articulates four voices of theology to be considered in the methodology of TAR: normative (Scripture and church teaching), formal (the work of theologians), operant (theology embedded in practice), and espoused (the stated beliefs of the community). In the context of sanctuary, normative theology includes but is not limited

---

55. Scharen, *Explorations in Ecclesiology*.

56. Helen Cameron, Deborah Bhatti, Catherine Duce, James Sweeney, and Clare Watkins, *Talking about God in Practice: Theological Action Research and Practical Theology* (London: SCM Press, 2010), 51, 54.

57. While the project has been guided by the theoretical commitments of TAR, particularly the four voices of theology, it has departed, in some ways, from the methodology laid out by Cameron et al. in *Talking about God*. The authors provide detailed guidelines for the formation of insider and outsider teams of theologians and practitioners. They also lay out guidelines on how to work together to formulate theological questions and interpret qualitative data. While my project emerged out of and relied on ongoing relationships with sanctuary practitioners, it did not follow all the guidelines of TAR.

to Christian social teaching and biblical mandates to welcome the stranger and protect the vulnerable. Formal theology related to sanctuary includes theologies of liberation, which emerge out of concrete praxis centered on a preferential option for the poor and marginalized. The themes of liberation theology were prominent in the espoused theologies of sanctuary, providing a faith-based rationale for accompaniment, political engagement, and public advocacy. The espoused and operant theologies of sanctuary, which do not always align, provide important resources for shaping and challenging formal and normative theologies.[58] Throughout this book, I examine sanctuary practices in conversation with Pope Francis's field hospital ecclesiology through a method of mutually critical correlation.

Specifically, I lift up Francis's field hospital church, informed by his social teaching, as a critical challenge to those sanctuary practices that do not include space-sharing; that is, those that emphasize the accompaniment of immigrants without considering the possibility of opening physical space-sharing, which has historically been a central practice of sanctuary. At the same time, I observe how sanctuary practices can inform, flesh out, and critically engage Francis's thought. I will argue that concrete sanctuary practices challenge Francis's dialectical understanding of space and time as well as gender and representation.

The orientation of the project, informed by my relationships with sanctuary leaders, involves building capacity for theological reflection within congregations and helping translate the theological underpinnings of sanctuary into public, accessible discourse. One of the ways TAR helps build capacity for theological reflection among faith communities is to help them identify how their espoused theology relates to operant theology. This motivation factored into my research as I observed barriers to solidarity, a central facet of the espoused theology of sanctuary practice that reflected and were reinforced by operant and normative ecclesiology of the community. Here again, I recognize the transformative potential of theology in practice to shape formal ecclesiology. Practices of solidarity in the sanctuary movement that are

---

58. Cameron et al., *Talking about God*, 56.

rooted in sustained encounter, mutual vulnerability, and story-sharing give rise to an ecclesiology of embodied solidarity that challenge the church to manifest the justice it proclaims.

The action-orientation of this project is rooted in my dual position vis-à-vis this work—as a researcher and as a practitioner. While my research questions influenced how I participated in sanctuary both within my own parish and in citywide efforts, my personal, faith-driven commitment to sanctuary also shaped my research. This interplay of identities—researcher, theologian, and Catholic—have shaped this work of ethnography and ecclesiology. Given this awareness, in addition to the qualitative methodology described below, I have employed what Emily Reimer-Barry has described as "empathetic listening"[59] as a foundation for ethnographically grounded theology.

Research Design

I focused specifically on San Francisco, initially on communities practicing sanctuary around immigration advocacy, which expanded to unhoused people. The decision to focus on San Francisco was motivated, in part, by my desire to explore how secular and religious notions of sanctuary exist alongside each other. Although the New Sanctuary Movement is interfaith and secular, I chose to limit my sample to Christian congregations, Protestant and Catholic, because I am particularly interested in articulating an ecclesiology of sanctuary from a Christian perspective. In a context marked by multiple ways of relating to faith and church-affiliation; however, this boundary cannot be neatly defined.

Because the people who officially represent churches are not necessarily the same people driving the sanctuary practice, I relied on relationships to identify key people to interview. Partners within the interfaith networks that coordinate sanctuary, particularly Faith in

59. Emily Reimer-Barry, "The Listening Church: How Ethnography Can Transform Catholic Ethics," in Vigen and Scharen, *Ethnography as Christian Theology*, 97–117, at 98.

Action and the Interfaith Movement for Human Integrity, along with people I met through my own participation in sanctuary-related events, provided an initial sample that grew as my network expanded. I wanted to achieve representation of all the Protestant and Catholic congregations that had declared sanctuary, while also connecting to churches who were actively discerning sanctuary or who were practicing accompaniment, advocacy, or space-sharing without a formal declaration of sanctuary.

The people I interviewed reflect the demographics of leadership in the sanctuary movement—the majority of whom were white, middle-aged, woman-identified, and middle- to upper-middle class. While the sample did include some racial and ethnic diversity, as well as diversity of gender, gender expression, and sexuality, the majority-white representation in sanctuary leadership is one of the barriers to solidarity I will address in the book. While I did not conduct formal interviews of recipients of sanctuary—immigrants or unhoused people—I listened to them in naturally occurring conversations during participant observation.

Two aspects of the project involved some level of participant observation: (1) a structured volunteer schedule at a church that provides sanctuary to unhoused people during the day and (2) a less-structured involvement in sanctuary for immigrants which emerged organically out of my prior participation in my parish. For two years, I participated in the sanctuary practice of my church, attending semi-regularly the church's "huddle for justice," in which the planning around accompaniment and advocacy occurred. I also attended immigration rallies and demonstrations through Faith in Action and the Interfaith Movement for Human Integrity. I took field notes immediately following these activities.

In order to understand sanctuary for unhoused people, I incorporated ongoing participant observation at a Catholic church in the Tenderloin who partners with the Gubbio Project[60] to welcome unhoused

---

60. The Gubbio Project is a nonprofit organization who partners with two San Francisco churches to support the practice of inviting unhoused people to sleep in the worship space during the day. Gubbio provides the staff, structure, and volunteers,

people to sleep in their pews each weekday morning. I participated as a volunteer, ritualizing hospitality near the door when people entered or exited the church and listening empathetically when people wanted to talk. I volunteered biweekly for five months,[61] with intermittent breaks, recording my observations immediately after my shift. I also interviewed staff and volunteers practicing this form of sanctuary at two sites in San Francisco.

The analysis of my interviews and fieldnotes incorporated principles of grounded theory, interpreting themes emergent from the data itself.[62] At the same time, I recognize that my insider-outsider perspective as a white, economically privileged, woman-identified theologian, as well as a practitioner of Catholicism and advocate for sanctuary, all factor into what I noticed and overlooked.

As I began paying more attention to concrete practices, I discovered how sanctuary seekers challenge categories of church-world, private-public, sacred-secular and construct sanctuary as an alternative space. The ecclesiological project that emerged attends to creative tensions embedded in these practices and presents a theology of the church rooted in the Christian narrative that embodies radical solidarity and disrupts neoliberal conceptions of private property. In other words, sanctuary offers an ecclesial embodiment of Pope Francis's social teaching, a concrete manifestation of the field hospital church.

---

while the church community provides the space. They describe their work as offering sanctuary. See https://www.thegubbioproject.org/, accessed on July 22, 2020.

61. The most consistent period of volunteering and observation was September 2019–January 2020. I intended to resume the schedule after a two-month break; however, social distancing regulations due to COVID-19 prevented me from doing so. I shifted the research design and conducted over twenty-five interviews with volunteers and staff members. I do not consider this a replacement of the participant observation I conducted but a shift in methodology necessitated by the unforeseeable reality of the pandemic.

62. My approach to writing and analyzing field notes has been informed by Robert Emerson, Rachel Fretz, and Linda Shaw, *Writing Ethnographic Fieldnotes* (Chicago: University of Chicago Press, 1995).

Structure of the Book

Chapter 1, "Searching for Sanctuary in the City of Saint Francis," highlights patterns of inclusion and exclusion in San Francisco as a context for faith-based expressions of sanctuary. The city of San Francisco is known for its progressive local politics, expressed concretely in its sanctuary ordinance. Beyond noninterference with federal immigration authorities, a number of faith communities in San Francisco collaborate with governmental and nongovernmental organizations to support immigrants and asylum seekers. Historically and today, the city offers a place of refuge for the LGBTQ community, which some faith leaders have described as a practice of sanctuary. Inclusion is a hallmark of sanctuary in San Francisco. At the same time, the growing economic inequality and housing crisis pushes residents out of the city or into the city streets, inviting a reflection on the significance of space in the practice of sanctuary. Reading this context through the social teaching of Pope Francis, who explicitly denounces a neoliberal view of private property and wealth, I highlight space as a site of ethical reflection. Francis envisions a church as a field hospital, one that goes forth toward the margins of society, prioritizes those who suffer, and prophetically witnesses to the joy of the Gospel. While Pope Francis's field hospital church offers a metaphor to move the church toward becoming sanctuary, Francis's dialectical understanding of other traditional binaries such as time and space, male and female, influence his ecclesiology in a way that hinders the embodied, concrete ecclesial praxis he prioritizes. The practiced ecclesiology of sanctuary, developed throughout the book, manifests a field hospital church that resists the polarization of process/space, binary power relations, and gendered dualism that reinforce a division of public and private spheres.

Chapter 2, "Sanctuary as Prophetic Witness," highlights sanctuary as ecclesial practices of accompaniment and public advocacy for immigrants. The majority of sanctuary congregations I studied prioritized accompaniment and advocacy but did not regard physical sanctuary as a possibility. In fact, it was not uncommon to assuage members who were on the fence about sanctuary that it did not involve the commitment to space-sharing. The practice of sanctuary among faith communities today is an outward movement, bringing the convictions of faith into the public sphere and challenging the relegation of faith to the private sphere. For these congregations, sanctuary provides an occasion to announce who they are or who they are becoming through performative social witness or an opportunity to reread their own history, articulating a narrative identity with public significance. Chapter 2 analyzes the exchange of meaning between faith communities and governmental and nongovernmental entities on sanctuary in San Francisco. Situating sanctuary practice within debates on public theology, it will expose the limitations of rational discourse to resist neoliberal notions of private property and argue for an ecclesial embodiment of radical solidarity.

The espoused theology of sanctuary embraces solidarity through accompaniment and advocacy. Yet barriers to solidarity exist within the sanctuary movement. An ongoing challenge is to empower recipients of sanctuary and recognize agency among those marginalized by racism, sexism, and poverty. Issues related to inclusion, agency, exploitation, and participation are reflected in ecclesial structures as well. Sanctuary declaration and practice reveals theological assumptions about the nature of the church: who speaks, who decides, and who does the messy work of accompaniment. Within this context, chapter 3, "Sanctuary as Embodied Solidarity," will explore barriers to sanctuary and, drawing upon a feminist ethic of risk, begin to articulate an ecclesiology that fosters the justice within the church itself so it can embody the solidarity it espouses.

Chapter 4, "Sanctuary as Sacramental Praxis," and chapter 5, "Sanctuary as Radical Hospitality," highlight a particular embodiment of sanctuary among unhoused people, one that disrupts notions of private and public, sacred and secular. The church provides the material backdrop of social practices that simultaneously reinforce and disrupt its sacred status. Chapter 4 explores how the space itself exercises an authority through evoking a sense of beauty or sense of spirituality, a contrast to religious institutions or state-run homeless shelters. Interrupting authorities of church and state, the sanctuary creates a thirdspace,[63] where relationships are transformed, and radical accompaniment is possible. Sanctuary expressed as a thirdspace, developed in chapter 5, challenges faith communities who emphasize sanctuary as public engagement to consider the significance of space as a resource for accompaniment and resistance. Drawing upon Catholic social teaching, this chapter will present faith-based sanctuary as a call for an embodied praxis that speaks to a secular context yet challenges a neoliberal model of private property.

This book ultimately develops an ecclesiology of sanctuary that challenges dominant assumptions about private property and retrieves the prophetic power of radical Christian hospitality. Embracing Pope Francis's image of the church as a field hospital, I argue that sanctuary practices reveal a church that is not only mobile and socially engaged but also one committed to holding space and embracing the messiness in the world in concrete practices of solidarity.

63. The concept of thirdspace, developed in postcolonial and feminist thought, is used here as a resource for spatial analysis. Edward Soja uses the concept to breakdown the binary approach to space as material/perceived or interpreted/conceived, observing how lived spaces are constructed through a complex interaction of identities. In doing so, he emphasizes how space is a site of contestation and negotiation of belonging. See Homi Bhabha, *The Location of Culture* (London: Routledge, 1994); Edward Soja, *Thirdspace: Journeys to Los Angeles and Other Real-and-Imagined Places* (Cambridge: Blackwell, 1996), bell hooks, *Yearning: Race, Gender, and Cultural Politics* (Boston: South End Press, 1990). See also *Thirdspace: A Journal of Feminist Theory & Culture.*

Chapter 1

Searching for Sanctuary in the City of St. Francis

S hortly after Cardinal Jorge Mario Bergoglio, SJ, of Argentina was elected pope, he told journalists why he chose Francis of Assisi as his namesake, "the man of poverty, the man of peace, the man who loves and protects creation. . . . How I would like a church that is poor and that is for the poor."[1] Francis has developed an ecclesiology of a poor church for the poor throughout his papacy, mostly through action and informal theological reflection in homilies, interviews, and audiences with people, many of whom are directly impacted by poverty.

In *Evangelii Gaudium*, his 2013 Apostolic Exhortation on the Joy of the Gospel, Francis presents "a church that goes forth."[2] He focuses consistently on the outward movement of the church, particularly toward the peripheries. Because Francis regards the structures of the church to be secondary to its social mission, he rejects a church that is focused inward. A self-referential, bureaucratic church "becomes sick," he argues:

---

1. Joshua McElwee, "Pope Francis: 'I Would Love a Church That Is Poor,'" *National Catholic Reporter*, March 16, 2013.

2. Pope Francis, Apostolic Exhortation on the Proclamation of the Gospel in Today's World, *Evangelii Gaudium*, www.vatican.va (2013), 46; cited hereafter as EG.

> I prefer a Church which is bruised, hurting, and dirty because
> it has been out on the streets, rather than a Church which is
> unhealthy from being confined and from clinging to its own
> security. I do not want a Church concerned with being at the
> center and which then ends by being caught up in a web of obses-
> sions and procedures.[3]

He offers an image of this bruised and dirty church who goes forth
to meet the needs of the world—a field hospital. Francis describes this
potent metaphor in an interview with Antonio Spadaro, SJ, in 2013:

> The thing the church needs most today is the ability to heal
> wounds and to warm the hearts of the faithful; it needs nearness,
> proximity. I see the church as a field hospital after battle. It is
> useless to ask a seriously injured person if he has high cholesterol
> and about the level of his blood sugars! You have to heal his
> wounds. Then we can talk about everything else. Heal the
> wounds, heal the wounds. . . . And you have to start from the
> ground up.[4]

This is not the only image Francis uses to describe the church, but the
field hospital provides a locus of reflection to understand and develop
his ecclesiology. I argue that this ecclesiology points to sanctuary as a
way of being church, not only an action of the church but a manifestation of an essential quality of "a poor church for the poor."

Although Francis does not use the language of sanctuary to describe
the social mission of the church, he has demonstrated through concrete
actions the practice of sanctuary as an essential quality of Christianity.
In 2015, over a million migrants entered Europe, most of whom were
Syrian asylum seekers fleeing a civil war. That year, Francis opened
the Vatican to shelter two refugee families and called upon the rest
of Europe to follow his example: "I address an appeal to the parishes,

---

3. EG, 49.

4. Pope Francis in an interview with Anthony Spadaro, "A Big Heart Open to
God," *America Magazine*, September 19, 2013.

to the religious communities, to the monasteries and shrines of all of Europe to express the concreteness of the Gospel and welcome a family of refugees."[5] He placed this concrete request within the context of the 2015 Year of Mercy. In the same spirit of mercy, he transformed Palazzo Migliori, a nineteenth-century palace that had been given to the Vatican, into a shelter for unhoused people. The beautiful sixteen-room "palace of the poor," managed by the St. Egidio community, is able to house up to fifty people. "Beauty heals," Francis said when he inaugurated the shelter and shared a meal with its residents.[6] Five years prior, Francis joined a group of unhoused neighbors for a private tour of the Sistine Chapel. He said of the beautiful, sacred space, "This is everyone's house, and your house. The doors are always open for all."[7]

San Francisco also bears the name of the great saint of the poor, a paradox given that it has the highest number of billionaires per capita of any US city.[8] Yet it is also home to one of the largest populations of unsheltered homeless people in the country.[9] The majority of un-housed residents live in district six, which includes the Tenderloin, a small neighborhood with a dense population, tight community, and high concentration of poverty. On the corner of Leavenworth and Golden Gate Avenue, the Franciscan-inspired St. Anthony Founda-tion is the largest multiservice provider to San Franciscans living in

5. Joshua McElwee, "Francis Calls on Every Parish across Europe to House Refu-gee Families," *National Catholic Reporter,* September 6, 2015.

6. Silvia Paggioli, "Pope Francis Turned a Vatican Palazzo into 'Palace of the Poor' for Homeless People," *National Public Radio,* February 7, 2020.

7. Cindy Wooden, "Pope Francis Joins Homeless People for Private Tour of Sistine Chapel," *National Catholic Reporter,* March 27, 2015.

8. Wealth-X annual "billionaire census" in 2018 reported one billionaire for every 11,600 residents of San Francisco, at https://www.wealthx.com/report/the-wealth-x -billionaire-census-2018/.

9. The 2019 point in time count lists just over eight thousand homeless people in San Francisco, 64 percent of whom were unsheltered, San Francisco Department of Homelessness and Supportive Housing. The percentage of unsheltered people expe-riencing homelessness per one hundred thousand residents was higher than New York; Boston; and Washington, DC; though their overall homeless population is greater. San Francisco City Performance Scorecards, Homelessness Benchmark, sfgov.org

poverty. Next door, St. Boniface Church, led by Franciscan brothers, opens its doors each morning so unhoused people can sleep in its pews. Like Pope Francis's palace of the poor, it provides not only space for rest but healing beauty.

Yet the Franciscan nomenclature scattered around the city also bears witness to the original displacement that marks the space. The Misión San Francisco de Asís, presently Mission Dolores, was founded by Franciscan priests on October 9, 1776, alongside the Presidio military settlement. Before European colonization, the area was home to communities of Native Californians known today as Ohlone.[10] This original displacement of Native Californians has been followed by successive displacement. The post–World War II Urban Renewal project uprooted over thirteen thousand mostly African American and Japanese American residents of the Fillmore–Western Addition neighborhood.[11] The influx of tech-driven wealth during the dot-com boom displaced working class people of color in neighborhoods such as the Mission District, now a textbook case of gentrification.[12]

As much as this city is marked by the dynamic of displacement, it has also been shaped by resistance to powers that exclude. Native Americans resisted cultural oppression by maintaining their language

10. Randall Milliken, Laurence E. Shoup, and Beverly Ortiz, "The Historic Indian People of California's San Francisco Peninsula—Draft Report." Submitted by Archaeological Consulting Services, Oakland, to National Park Service, Golden Gate Recreation Area, San Francisco, 2005. Barbara L. Voss, *The Archaeology of Ethnogenesis: Race and Sexuality in Colonial San Francisco*, rev. ed. (Gainsville: University Press of Florida, 2015), 47.

11. Clement Lai, "The Racial Triangulation of Space: The Case of Urban Renewal in San Francisco's Fillmore District," *Annals of the Association of American Geographers* 102, no. 1 (2012): 151–170, 160.

12. Sydney Cespedes, Mitchell Crispell, Christina Blackston, Jonathan Plowman, and Edward Graves, The Center for Community Innovation (CCI) at UC-Berkeley and People Organizing to Demand Environmental & Economic Rights (PODER), "Mission: Community Organizing and Resistance in SF's Mission District," Case Study on Gentrification and Displacement Pressures in the Mission District of San Francisco, California (June 2015), at http://iurd.berkeley.edu/uploads/Mission_District_Final.pdf..

and traditions that had been suppressed through colonization.[13] Likewise, when the city began condemning and destroying homes as part of its redevelopment strategy, residents resisted, forming the Western Addition Community Organization (WACO).[14] Similarly, the Mission Coalition Organization mobilized a diverse group against redevelopment plans in the Mission District.[15] Today the groups Eviction Free San Francisco and Anti-Eviction Mapping Project resist the hyper-gentrification driven by the tech boom 2.0.[16] Urban affairs scholar Rachel Brahinsky highlights antidisplacement movements to counter the narrative that gentrification is inevitable.[17]

Brahinsky and others point to sources of resistance to gentrification that make up the city's unique activist, antiestablishment culture shaped by a history of social movements for LGBTQ rights, tenants' rights, environmentalism, and slow growth. The city's sanctuary status is readily associated with its progressive "left coast" identity. However,

13. Brooke S. Arkush, "Native Responses to European Intrusion: Cultural Persistence and Agency among Mission Neophytes in Spanish Colonial Northern California," *Historical Archaeology* 45, no. 4 (2011): 62–90. Learn about the history and culture of the Ramaytush Ohlone (https://www.ramaytush.com/) and Muwekma Ohlone (http://www.muwekma.org/) who trace their ancestry to the San Francisco region.

14. Lai, "The Racial Triangulation of Space,"151.

15. Mike Miller, "People Power in San Francisco: The Mission Coalition," *Race, Poverty & the Environment: Reimagine! Who Owns Our Cities?* 15, no. 1 (Spring 2008): 65–67.

16. Florian Opillard, "Resisting the Politics of Displacement in the San Francisco Bay Area: Anti-Gentrification Activism in the Tech Boom 2.0," *European Journal of American Studies* 10, no. 3 (2015): 1–23. Hyper-gentrification, according to Jeremiah Moss, also described as "fourth wave" gentrification (Loretta Lees), refers to state-supported urban transformation to appeal to global corporate interests. Moss argues that neoliberalism is "the invisible engine that drives hyper-gentrification" (*Vanishing New York: How a Great City Lost its Soul* [New York: HarperCollins, 2017], 103).

17. Rachel Brahinsky, "The Story of Property: Meditations on Gentrification, Renaming, and Possibility," *Environment and Planning A: Economy and Space* 52, no. 5 (January 2020): 837–55. She challenges the thesis put forth by Smith and Hackworth that third-wave gentrification, global in nature, was largely uncontested. See also Jason Hackworth and Neil Smith, "The Changing State of Gentrification," *Tijdschrift voor Economische en Sociale Geografie* 92, no. 4 (2001): 464–77.

progressive culture and politics do not necessarily generate inclusion. In fact, as Brahinsky points out, "the liberal drive to make cities more appealing also tends to make them more exclusive—at the expense of the liberal/progressive goal of social inclusiveness."[18] Environmentalists and slow-growth advocates resist capitalist-driven urban change, while also, however, stunting initiatives that some argue could address the city's housing crisis.

So, while the city's cultural-ethnic diversity, progressive immigration courts, and liberal political stances on immigrant rights, LGBTQ rights, and workers' rights are all assets in making San Francisco a sanctuary city, it is not enough to create the kind of inclusion that sanctuary, historically, theologically, and ethically implies. Historically, the practice of sanctuary has set spaces apart to resist exclusion. Whether designated for criminals, runaway slaves, or refugees, sanctuary is created around the basic premise that those who are marginalized or persecuted have a place in community. Sanctuary, as a radical practice of space-sharing subverts the idea that private property is an absolute right, making it a powerful tool to contest the neoliberal ideologies shaping urban centers today.[19] While some faith communities and activists stress the interconnections of immigration advocacy and San Francisco's crisis of affordable housing and homelessness, space-sharing emerges as a less utilized practice in the New Sanctuary Movement. Reflecting theologically on sanctuary as a way of being church challenges faith communities to practice sanctuary as a way to resist a neoliberal understanding of property and space.

---

18. Rachel Brahinsky, *The Making and Unmaking of Southeast San Francisco* (PhD diss., University of California, Berkeley, 2012), 9. Richard DeLeon unpacks San Francisco's progressivism, pointing to distinctive coalitions dedicated in different ways to slow growth in the face of the city's post–World War II aim to redevelop the city into a financial center. Richard DeLeon *Left Coast City: Progressive Politics in San Francisco, 1975–1991* (Lawrence: University Press of Kansas, 1992).

19. Later in the chapter, I elaborate on this observation made by David Harvey and Neil Smith that connects urban transformation and neoliberalism. See David Harvey, *Spaces of Neoliberalization: Towards a Theory of Uneven Geographical Development* (Stuttgart: Franz Steiner Verlag, 2005); Neil Smith, *The New Urban Frontier: Gentrification and the Revanchist City* (London: Routledge, 1996).

Without naming it as sanctuary, Pope Francis has offered an understanding of church that makes concrete his strong critique of a neoliberal "idolatry of money." Francis's understanding of the social mission of the church provides a critical framework for analyzing sanctuary in San Francisco. In this chapter, I will begin to develop key aspects of an ecclesiology of sanctuary in conversation with Pope Francis's image of the church as a field hospital. First, I examine the dynamics of inclusion and exclusion in San Francisco, arguing that sanctuary rooted in Christian theology must include a concrete commitment to space-sharing with those who have been marginalized by unjust systems, including what Francis describes as "an economy that kills." Then I explore the social teaching of Pope Francis, which provides the skeleton for his field hospital ecclesiology. Pope Francis interprets Catholic social thought using spatial metaphors of exclusion, inclusion, peripheries, and margins. Integrating the theme and explicit language of the preferential option for the poor into the papal social teaching, Francis builds his ecclesiology around the social mandate to prioritize people on the peripheries.[20] At the end of the chapter, I signal a critical engagement with Francis's thought that will frame the remainder of the book. Specifically, I examine Francis's commitment to the idea that "time is greater than space." Rooted in a dialectical epistemology, this commitment will be challenged by those who recognize space as socially constructed.[21] Here, the theology of sanctuary emerging out of concrete practices will challenge, illuminate, and reinforce aspects of Francis's ecclesiology, while his formal ecclesiology will also challenge, illuminate, and reinforce theologies in practice.

---

20. Andrea Riccardi explains the centrality of geographical metaphors in Francis's teaching: "the church's so-called 'option for the poor' is its true historical and geographical task. . . . Of course the poor and the marginalized overlap and are the same people, but we should note that the use of the geographical expression marginal has a particular connotation in the pope's language" (*To the Margins: Pope Francis and the Mission of the Church* [Maryknoll, NY: Orbis, 2018], introduction).

21. Doreen Massey, "Philosophy and Politics of Spatiality: Some Considerations, The Hettner-Lecture in Human Geography," *Geographische Zeitschrift* 87, no. 1 (1999): 1–12; Edward Soja, *Thirdspace: Journeys to Los Angeles and Other Real-and-Imagined Places* (Oxford: Blackwell Publishers, 1996).

Inclusion and Exclusion in San Francisco

Naming the tensions that mark San Francisco as a sanctuary city and global city,[22] politics scholar Keally McBride writes, "there is a strong case to be made for the dismissal of the sanctuary practices and supposed progressivism of San Francisco as a flimsy scrim. . . . Of course it is safe to invite folks to come sit at your table if there is no practical way for them to make it to your house."[23] McBride does not dismiss San Francisco's sanctuary status so readily, observing a progressive political culture that still exists, albeit in tension with the neoliberal pattern of development and gentrification that has shaped San Francisco, similarly to New York and other global cities. But she makes an important point about the challenge of being a sanctuary city and a global financial center. San Francisco is a sanctuary for those who have left everything behind with the hope of a better life, but once they arrive, they face an average rent of over $3000 for a one-bedroom apartment.[24] Reflecting on the impact of gentrification, Richard Walker writes "outcast youth today are more likely to be homeless than bohemian. Wages and union strength have eroded, and the working class has been recomposed as

22. Global cities, described by Saskia Sassen, are transnational urban centers that concentrate information and capital within the network of other powerful cities. Enabled by economic globalization, these corporate headquarters become increasingly "disconnected from their broader hinterlands and even national economies" and "the growing numbers of high-level professionals and high profit-making specialized service firms have the effect of raising the degree of spatial and socio-economic inequality evident in these cities" ("Global City: Introducing a Concept," *The Brown Journal of World Affairs* 11, no. 2 [Winter/Spring 2005]: 30).

23. Keally McBride, "Sanctuary San Francisco: Recent Developments in Local Sovereignty and Spatial Politics," *Theory & Event* 12, no. 4 (2009), https://muse.jhu.edu/article/368574.

24. This reflects the average rent at the time I started this project (2017). The average rent of a one-bedroom apartment in San Francisco dropped 23.2 percent during the COVID-19 pandemic but is beginning to increase again to $2,082 as I conclude this project in March 2021. San Francisco rent report provided by Apartment List (April 2021), available at https://www.apartmentlist.com/ca/san-francisco#rent-report.

largely foreign-born Asian and Latin peoples who face greater obstacles than their white predecessors."[25]

This section will explore what it means to be a sanctuary city and how the municipal commitment relates to faith-driven sanctuary practices. I will focus initially on San Francisco as a sanctuary city defined by its pro-immigration policies before considering the broader ways San Francisco has been a sanctuary to other marginalized communities. Taking seriously McBride's observation, I will examine paradox of being a sanctuary city marked by economic inequality, gentrification, and homelessness.

A Sanctuary City

San Francisco became a sanctuary city with the passing of the "City of Refuge" resolution in 1985 and ordinance in 1989. In this context, sanctuary primarily refers to the city's refusal to commit local law enforcement to assist federal immigration authorities. San Francisco's sanctuary ordinance also includes the requirement for municipal workers to provide city services to all residents, regardless of immigration status.[26] Sanctuary cities have grown in number today, and with the passing of the "California Values Act" SB 54 in 2017, California became a sanctuary state. Sanctuary municipalities have increasingly become symbols of progressive politics, particularly as the Trump administration has targeted them as threats to his vision of national security.

Peter Mancina has well documented the critical role faith communities played in shaping the sanctuary movement that led to the municipal identity and declaration. Churches and synagogues retrieved the language of sanctuary to name the practice of providing refuge to Salvadoran and Guatemalan migrants routinely denied asylum in the

25. Richard Walker, "An Appetite for the City," in *Reclaiming San Francisco: History, Politics, Culture*, ed. James Brook, Chris Carlsson, and Nancy J. Peters (San Francisco: City Lights Books, 1998), 16.

26. Peter Mancina, "The Birth of a Sanctuary-City: A History of Governmental Sanctuary in San Francisco," in *Sanctuary Practices in International Perspectives: Migration, Citizenship, and Social Movements*, ed. Randy Lippert and Sean Rehagg (London: Routledge, 2013).

1980s. This was accompanied by public advocacy and civil disobedience against the US government's foreign policy toward Central America.[27] In partnership with community organizers and with the support of prominent religious leader and Catholic archbishop John Quinn, sanctuary workers translated Scripture and liberation theology into an ethical vision that resonated with progressive members of the city's Board of Supervisors.[28] The sanctuary declaration emerged out of a convergence of the faith-driven commitment toward transnational solidarity and San Francisco's identity as a progressive city marked by inclusion of those excluded elsewhere in the United States.

San Francisco has also defied dominant US culture and state and federal laws that discriminate against those who identify as LGBTQ. In 2004, the city started issuing marriage licenses to same-sex couples before the state of California legalized same-sex marriage in 2013, and finally, the US Supreme Court in 2015 granted legal recognition of same-sex couples as a constitutional right. At the time, then-mayor Gavin Newsom set San Francisco apart as a sanctuary for the LGBTQ community, defending the sovereignty of the city against what many perceived as unjust and unconstitutional laws. While some faith communities have opposed San Francisco's inclusive stance toward the LGBTQ community, other progressive churches have been allies, sometimes in opposition to their official leaders.[29]

Rebecca Solnit describes San Francisco as a sanctuary in a broad sense, pointing to its inclusion of other marginalized groups, namely, "the queer, the eccentric, the creative, the radical, the political and

27. Susan Bibler Coutin, *The Culture of Protest: Religious Activism and the U.S. Sanctuary Movement* (Boulder: Westview Press, 1993).

28. Mancina, "The Birth of a Sanctuary-City."

29. Donal Godfrey describes how Most Holy Redeemer Catholic Church became a sanctuary for the LGBTQ community. Gay activists and allies transformed it into a safe space, not only from the hostile society but also from a church that marginalizes LGBTQ people through its official theology and practice. See Donal Godfrey, *Gays and Grays: The Story of the Inclusion of the Gay Community at Most Holy Redeemer Catholic Parish in San Francisco* (Landham: Lexington, 2007).

economic refugees."[30] The antiestablishment, contrarian culture that emerged from within the city made it appealing to other groups who found themselves outside of mainstream American culture in the 1960s. During this period, San Francisco was the "countercultural capital of postwar America" Richard Walker describes, and for many people "the city itself was an object of celebration as well as liberation."[31] However, Solnit fears that San Francisco is losing its uniquely inclusive and diverse quality as gentrification displaces activists, artists, and working-class citizens.

San Francisco's prolabor history has been a crucial aspect of its resistance to displacement. Powerful unions such as the International Association of Longshoremen were integral to the city's economy in the early twentieth century. Faith-based activism had an important role in organizing workers around their rights. William Issel highlights the impact of Catholic social teaching on San Francisco's prolabor activism, which mobilized San Francisco's working class in the first half of the twentieth century.[32] And while San Francisco still boasts local laws to protect the working class and poor not seen in other US cities—mandatory paid sick days, health care for all, a city-based minimum wage—the economy has changed the city in ways that mimic other global cities. By the mid-1970s, blue collar jobs had declined, while the jobs in finance, real estate, and insurance grew. Today, many working class and poor people find jobs in the informal economy as domestic workers, Lyft drivers, or Instacart shoppers. Chris Carlsson remarks, "San Francisco's once-vaunted labor movement at the end of the twentieth century has been reduced to whispering where it once roared."[33]

30. Rebecca Solnit, *Hollow City: The Siege of San Francisco and the Crisis of American Urbanism* (New York: Verso, 2000), 30–31.

31. Walker, "An Appetite for the City," 12.

32. William Issel, *Church and State in the City: Catholics and Politics in Twentieth-Century San Francisco* (Philadelphia: Temple University Press, 2012).

33. Chris Carlsson, "The Progress Club 1934 and Class Memory," in *Reclaiming San Francisco*, 68.

An Exclusive City

San Francisco's transformation in the past forty years has followed a pattern similar to other global cities such as New York, while also reflecting the uniqueness of its space, local politics, history, and culture. Geographer David Harvey describes how cities have transformed in response to neoliberalism. Although neoliberalism as an ideology rests on the assumption that the state should step back to promote the freedom of the market, Harvey describes how city governments actively support neoliberalism by becoming "entrepreneurs" in order to compete within a global economy.[34] Within this model, cities must make spatial changes to attract tourists, private investors, and white-collar workers. Concretely, these changes fuel gentrification.

Jason Hackworth and Neil Smith identified stages of gentrification in their study of New York City. They observe a movement from sporadic gentrification in the 1960s, which intensified in the 1980s in city-center neighborhoods, toward a postrecession third wave, which is more clearly linked to large-scale capital, as state-supported developers transform entire neighborhoods.[35] Hackworth and Smith argue that we are living in a period marked by "generalized gentrification," which is more state-facilitated as city governments privatize services and partner with investors to develop the city to meet the demands of the global market. Gentrification in this context is not random but follows a "global strategy," creating financial "command centers" that promote capitalist production. Hackworth and Smith explicitly connect urban change and globalization to neoliberalism, which they characterize as a return to the basic assumptions of eighteenth-century liberalism—that individual self-interest is the foundation of democracy, private property expresses self-interest, and the free market is the best way to exchange it. In another article, Smith goes on to argue that, unlike the liberalism of the past, neoliberalism is "galvanized by an unprecedented mobiliza-

34. David Harvey, "From Managerialism to Entrepreneurialism: The Transformation in Urban Governance in Late Capitalism," *Geografiska Annaler* 71, no. 1 (1989): 3–17.

35. Jason Hackworth and Neil Smith, "The Changing State of Gentrification," *Tijdschrift voor Economische en Sociale Geografie*, 92, no. 4 (2001): 464–77.

tion not just of national state power but of state power organized and exercised at different geographic scales."[36]

San Franciscans long-resisted the "Manhattanization" of the city, advocating for slow growth.[37] Despite the resistance, San Francisco followed a similar pattern of state-supported gentrification observed by Smith. The expansion of downtown office buildings prevailed in the 1980s, solidifying San Francisco alongside New York as the center of US commerce.[38] San Francisco's geographic location made it particularly attractive to corporations that wanted to capitalize on growing trade opportunities within the Pacific Rim.[39] The city was a willing partner in redeveloping downtown and South of Market regions to promote business interests, Chester Hartman argues. Corporate representatives populated planning councils and committees aimed at development of real estate and transportation. Hartman concludes that "San Francisco city government overall has been extremely supportive of what the corporate community wants to do with and to the city."[40]

During the dot-com era of the 1990s and tech boom of the 2000s, Democratic pro-development mayors, Willie Brown and Edwin Lee respectively, promoted the transformation of the city in ways that critics argue have advanced the interests of big business. A concrete example of pro-corporate politics is the Twitter tax break of 2011. Officially called the Central Market Street and Tenderloin Area Payroll Expense Tax Exclusion, it encouraged companies to move headquarters to downtown San Francisco by exempting them from the city's 1.5 percent payroll tax. Unemployment fell, more professionals moved into the city, and private sector business grew during the period between

36. Neil Smith, "New Globalism, New Urbanism: Gentrification as Global Urban Strategy," *Antipode* 34, no. 3 (2002): 427–50, at 429.

37. DeLeon, *Left Coast City.*

38. Chester Hartman with Sarah Carnochan, *City for Sale: The Transformation of San Francisco,* rev. ed. (Oakland: University of California Press, 2002).

39. Hartman, *City for Sale.*

40. Hartman, *City for Sale,* 394.

2011–2017.[41] However, the homeless population in the nearby Tenderloin district also grew, along with complaints about the visibility of street homelessness.[42]

The redevelopment of downtown and South of Market has coincided with strategies to deter visible homelessness. This includes quality-of-life laws that disproportionately impact unhoused people, such as laws prohibiting panhandling and sleeping and loitering in public spaces.[43] Under Mayors Mark Farrell and London Breed, the city ramped up its enforcement of Proposition Q (2016), which banned tents on the sidewalk. This has resulted in the confiscation of property through regular sweeps of homeless encampments by the SF Department of Public Works.[44] San Francisco's Department of Homelessness and Supportive Housing, along with advocacy groups such as the Coalition on Homelessness, have demonstrated that these strategies fail to address the most commonly reported cause of homelessness—the cost of housing in San Francisco.[45]

Today, San Francisco has one of the highest costs of living among US metro areas[46] and one of the widest gaps between the wealthy and

41. Trisha Thadani, "Winners, Losers—or Both?" *San Francisco Chronicle*, May 9, 2019, https://projects.sfchronicle.com/2019/mid-market/city/.

42. Thadani, "Winners, Losers—or Both?"

43. A 2016 report by the San Francisco Budget and Analyst Office documented that the city spent $20.6 million in 2015 for sanctioning homeless people—for violating quality of life laws. For an analysis of San Francisco's strategy to address homelessness see Stacey Murphy, "'Compassionate' Strategies of Managing Homelessness: Post-Revanchist Geographies in San Francisco," *Antipode* 41, no. 2 (March 2009): 305–25.

44. Nuala Sawyer, "Sweeps of Homeless Camps in S.F. Are Creating a Public Health Crisis" *Blog for the Center for Health Journalism at University of Southern California*, March 21, 2019, at https://centerforhealthjournalism.org/2019/03/14/sweeps -homeless-camps-sf-are-creating-public-health-crisis.

45. SF Department of Homelessness and Supportive Housing HUD point-in-time count report for 2019. Coalition on Homelessness fact sheet on homelessness (2019), at http://www.cohsf.org/wp-content/uploads/2019/10/Fact-Sheet-on-Homelessness -2019.pdf.

46. The Economic Policy Institute's "Family Budget Calculator" estimates that a family of four needs to make a minimum annual income of $148,440 for a "modest

impoverished.[47] The San Francisco housing market has increasingly favored the wealthy, with average rents increasing around 40 percent between 2010 and 2018.[48] This has occurred alongside successive increases of reported evictions during the same period.[49] Neighborhoods such as the Mission District have undergone rapid gentrification as tech professionals have moved into the city to meet the industry demand. This has been matched by anti-eviction activism across the city.[50] In 2013 and again in 2018, protesters focused on stopping Google buses from crowding the city bus stops. The Google bus protests became symbolic of the city's catering to tech professionals over services such as public transportation, which are supposed to benefit everyone. Although antitech protests have drawn attention to the problem of displacement, Rachel Brahinsky cautions against blaming "techies" for the larger problem of hyper-gentrification, marked by rapid displacement through eviction and rising housing costs. The San Francisco Bay Area, she argues, needs a true "ethical urbanism" that involves the development of affordable housing without displacement, greater

yet adequate" standard of living in San Francisco, at https://www.epi.org/resources/budget/.

47. The Public Policy Institute of California analyzes the income distribution in the Bay Area, noting that the top 10 percent of earners make 12.2 times more than the bottom 10 percent ($384,000 versus $32,000, respectively), at https://www.ppic.org/publication/income-inequality-in-california/.

48. Although the US Census notes an increase in average rent of $1058 in 2010 to $1880 in 2018, this does not reflect the dramatic increase for new renters. Trulia notes a 37.9 percent increase between 2012 and 2018, and Real Page reports a 48.6 percent increase from 2010 to 2019. Adam Brinklow, "This Decade, San Francisco Saw the End of Renting as We Know It," *Curbed San Francisco*, December 12, 2019, at https://sf.curbed.com/2019/12/12/21001080/san-francisco-sf-rent-prices-end-decade-2010s.

49. San Francisco Rent Board, "Special Eviction Report—Twenty Years of Rent Board Annual Reports on Eviction Notices 1997–2017," sfrb.org.

50. Florian Opillard, "Resisting the Politics of Displacement in the San Francisco Bay Area: Anti-Gentrification Activism in the Tech Boom 2.0," *European Journal of American Studies* 10, no. 3 (2015): 1–23.

accountability to uphold tenants' rights, and more transparency about the rate of evictions.[51]

Just as faith communities informed the city's pro-immigrant sanctuary commitment, I argue that they have a critical role in resisting the ongoing dynamics of exclusion in San Francisco to make it a true sanctuary for all. Sanctuary rooted in a theology and practice of radical hospitality and solidarity with the excluded goes beyond a liberal public identity or commitment to noninterference. Particularly in a context in which space is a site of contestation, where the dynamics of inclusion and exclusion play out in such prominent ways, sanctuary must involve an ethical reflection on private property. Sanctuary as space-sharing offers a visible critique of neoliberalism and the large-scale inequality it perpetuates. The ecclesiology developed by Pope Francis, rooted in his social vision that prioritizes those on the periphery, offers a concrete theology of sanctuary.[52]

Inclusion and Exclusion in Pope Francis's Social Teaching

Exclusion: Idolatry of Money Fuels a Throw-Away Culture

In a June 5, 2013, general audience in St. Peter's Square, Pope Francis said:

> Men and women are sacrificed to the idols of money and consumption. That some homeless people freeze to death on the street, that is not news. On the other hand, a drop of 10 points

---

51. Rachel Brahinsky, "The Death of the City? Reports of San Francisco's Demise Have Been Greatly Exaggerated," *Boom: A Journal of California* 4, no. 2 (2014): 43–54.

52. I do not mean to present this theology of sanctuary as exhaustive of all approaches, recognizing how other traditions—religious and secular—conceive of sanctuary and practice it historically. Christian practices of sanctuary are not neatly delineated from non-Christian practices. However, my intention is to construct an ecclesiology of sanctuary informed by concrete practices in conversation with formal theology and ethics from Christian perspectives, with particular attention to the thought of Pope Francis.

in the stock markets of some cities is a tragedy. That is how people are thrown away. We, people, are thrown away, as if we were trash.[53]

He could have been speaking directly to San Francisco, where an estimated 240 people died on the streets in 2018.[54] This quote reveals much about Francis's social teaching, which directly informs his ecclesiology. The dynamic of exclusion and inclusion frames Francis's social teaching, which is both rooted in the larger Catholic social tradition and unique in style and substance. For Francis, the idolatry of money fuels a throw-away culture that excludes the poor and oppressed. A throw-away culture is sustained by indifference toward suffering of the marginalized, which must be overcome through closeness to the poor, by going to the margins to encounter and be transformed by compassion. Francis does not just speak of the poor, but directly with them. He goes out to the streets, shelters, and border towns receiving refugees and challenges the world to solidarity. He dreams of a field hospital church that does the same.

Pope Francis evokes the image of people literally dying on the streets to make a moral argument against an economic system and related culture that perpetuates exclusion. Francis eschews theoretical and abstract language in his social teaching, pointing instead to the material reality of poverty. In his exhortation Joy of the Gospel, Francis highlights what he considers to be the challenges of today's world. Top on the list is an economy that kills: "Just as the commandment 'Thou shalt not kill' sets a clear limit in order to safeguard the value of

53. Pope Francis, General Audience at St. Peter's Square, June 5, 2013, at http://www.vatican.va/content/francesco/en/audiences/2013/documents/papa-francesco_20130605_udienza-generale.html.

54. The San Francisco Department of Public Health reported 135 deaths (Barry Zevin, MD, and Caroline Cawley, MPH, San Francisco Whole Person Care, "Homeless Mortality in San Francisco: Opportunities for Prevention" [February 19, 2019]). The community's count, led by the Coalition on Homelessness, was higher at 240 (Ida Mojadad, "Homeless Persons Vigil Remembers Those Lost on S.F. Streets" *SF Weekly*, December 16, 2019).

human life, today we also have to say 'thou shalt not' to an economy of exclusion and inequality. Such an economy kills."[55]

Francis is very concrete in naming ways the global economy kills, highlighting inequality and exclusion, not just poverty, as the sources of violence. He points out that people starve to death—not because there is not enough food in the world but because of unequal distribution. People with excess throw food away, while others lack basic needs.[56] In his address to the World Gathering of Popular Movements in Bolivia, Francis refers to ways the global economy threatens the livelihood of farmworkers, pointing to loss of land, agricultural work, and sustenance due to the "frenetic levels" of consumption.[57] He recognizes that severe inequality cultivates social unrest, echoing Paul VI's observation in *Populorum Progressio* that when people are oppressed, violence is a temptation. Francis further challenges people who blame the poor for violence in their communities by emphasizing social sin, "If every action has its consequences, an evil embedded in the structures of a society has a constant potential for disintegration and death. It is evil crystallized in unjust social structures, which cannot be the basis of hope for a better future."[58]

The pope clearly and consistently links economic inequality and related injustices to a cultural ethos shaped by consumerism. This is not new to Catholic social thought. Early Catholic social thought defended the universal purpose of created goods, arguing that individuals were obligated to give out of their surplus. John Paul II developed this further, beyond individual choices, by denouncing consumerism as endemic to a "culture of death," which values people based on their

---

55. EG, 53.

56. EG, 53.

57. Pope Francis, Address to Participants in the World Meeting of Popular Movements (October 28, 2014), at http://www.vatican.va/content/francesco/en/speeches/2014/october/documents/papa-francesco_20141028_incontro-mondiale-movimenti-popolari.html.

58. EG, 59.

productivity and celebrates "having" over "being."[59] When the human person is reduced to their role in economic production and consumption, those who are elderly, young, or live with a disability are deemed less valuable and are even discarded. John Paul II and Francis both link this cultural ethos to social inequalities.

Francis is less ambiguous than John Paul II,[60] however, in his insistence that consumerism is not only a problem of how people relate to money or possessions. For Francis, consumerism is inextricably linked to the system of neoliberal capitalism, which he firmly rejects:

> As long as the problems of the poor are not radically resolved by rejecting the absolute autonomy of markets and financial speculation and by attacking the structural causes of inequality, no solution will be found for the world's problems, or, for that matter, to any problems. Inequality is the *root of social ills* (emphasis added).[61]

Thomas Massaro notes the significance of Francis's emphasis on inequality as the root of social ills. By going beyond the problem of poverty, Francis recognizes how power operates in economic and social systems. This is significant, Massaro argues, because Catholic social thought has at times preferred to emphasize social harmony over conflict and has been critiqued for failing to give sufficient attention to power. Francis clearly recognizes that inequality serves the interests of people with power, while it marginalizes the poor. The influence of liberation theology has been well-documented in Francis's thought,

59. John Paul II described a culture of death in *Evangelium Vitae* (1995) and elaborated a critique of a consumer attitude that values having over being in his encyclical "On the Hundredth Anniversary of Rerum Novarum" *Centesimus Annus* (May 1, 1991), 36; cited hereafter as CA.

60. Michael Novak has interpreted John Paul II's social teaching in favor of the free market. Yet Todd Whitmore effectively challenges Novak's interpretation by pointing out key theological differences in "John Paul II, Michael Novak, and the Differences between Them," (*The Annual of the Society of Christian Ethics* 21 [January 2001]: 215–32).

61. EG, 202.

even though the pope avoids explicit Marxist theory as a framework. Massaro notes that Francis names and rejects the same dynamic of center-periphery at the heart of Marxist thought, but he prefers non-theoretical, practical language in his moral arguments.[62]

Francis exemplifies this practical, pastoral, persuasive approach in his 2020 encyclical on social friendship, *Fratelli Tutti*. Written in the midst of the COVID-19 global pandemic, Francis invites the reader into the story of the Good Samaritan to prompt moral discernment and self-examination. Through his commentary on the story, Francis challenges the reader to recognize their obligation toward their neighbor, with an ever-expanding understanding of who one's neighbor is— beyond their immediate family and neighborhood, beyond national borders. Francis uses the story to denounce indifference toward the poor and marginalized by those who limit their scope of interest to their own well-being.[63] Connecting consumerism and individualism to the decline of community life needed to address the social ills exacerbated by the pandemic, Francis offers one of his strongest critiques of neoliberalism to date. Specifically, he argues, "The marketplace, by itself, cannot resolve every problem, however much we are asked to believe this dogma of neoliberal faith."[64]

This statement echoes a consistent theme in Francis's thought—when profit is the sole purpose of the market, it functions as an idol. Francis names a contradiction that free markets do not lead to free participation in society. Not only does Francis consider the poor to be unfree because of oppressive inequality, but he also recognizes how people with wealth and power are unfree because the drive to possess is unrelenting. "The thirst for power and possessions knows no limits. In this system, which tends to devour everything which stands in the way of increased profits,

---

62. Thomas Massaro, "Pope Francis on Overcoming Exclusion: A Theological Vision with Economic and Social Implications," *American Journal of Economics and Sociology* 78, no. 4 (September 2019): 865–93.

63. Pope Francis, Encyclical Letter on Fraternity and Social Friendship, *Fratelli Tutti* (October 3, 2020), chapter 2; cited hereafter as FT.

64. FT, 168.

whatever is fragile, like the environment, is defenseless before the interests of a deified market, which become the only rule."[65]

Although he is greatly concerned with the accumulation of wealth, Francis does not outright reject private ownership. Embracing the theological vision of the universal purpose of created goods, Catholic social thought considers private property as a right alongside the responsibility to the common good. John Paul II emphasized this point by claiming that private property is under a social mortgage.[66] Pope Francis, more than John Paul II, emphasizes the limits of private property because, while John Paul was particularly sensitive to excessive centralization under communism, Francis has witnessed how the concentration of wealth in the hands of few perpetuates exclusion.

For Pope Francis, consumerism is so pernicious because it objectifies people and undermines the foundational conviction in Catholic social thought that human dignity is intrinsic and establishes a person's inalienable worth. Consumerism, Francis argues, assigns value to a person based on their contribution to the economic system, leading to a particularly profound type of exclusion:

> Human beings are themselves considered consumer goods to be used and then discarded. We have created a "throw away" culture which is now spreading. It is no longer simply about exploitation and oppression, but something new. Exclusion ultimately has to do with what it means to be a part of the society in which we live; those excluded are no longer society's underside or its fringes or its disenfranchised—they are no longer even a part of it. The excluded are not the "exploited" but the outcast, the "leftovers."[67]

Here we can better understand Francis's notion of the periphery to which the church must go. The extreme form of exclusion perpetuated by a throw-away culture and idolatry of money renders people invisible

---

65. EG, 56.

66. John Paul II, "On Social Concern" *Sollicitudo Rei Socialis* (December 30, 1987), 42; cited hereafter as SRS.

67. EG, 53.

to the dominant society. San Francisco, like other cities, is set up to contain the unwanted features of urban life—poverty, drug use, homelessness—so they are invisible to nonpoor residents, tourists, and investors. But as Francis has argued, this perpetuates indifference toward the suffering of those who are disenfranchised. Indifference is a barrier to solidarity and encounter is the antidote. Through his teaching and actions, Francis demonstrates solidarity with the excluded, calling the world to overcome indifference and build structures of inclusion.

Encounter: Closeness with the Poor Overcomes a Culture of Indifference

In his first trip outside of Rome, Francis visited the Italian island of Lampedusa. He spoke among a crowd of migrants, but his audience extended far beyond the people attending:

> But I would like us to ask a third question: "Has any one of us wept because of this situation and others like it?" Has any one of us grieved for the death of these brothers and sisters? Has any one of us wept for these persons who were on the boat? For the young mothers carrying their babies? For these men who were looking for a means of supporting their families? We are a society which has forgotten how to weep, how to experience compassion—"suffering with" others: the globalization of indifference has taken from us the ability to weep! . . . let us ask the Lord for the grace to weep over our indifference, to weep over the cruelty of our world, of our own hearts, and of all those who in anonymity make social and economic decisions which open the door to tragic situations like this. "Has any one wept?" Today has anyone wept in our world?[68]

Francis's call to solidarity flows from a theological and social tradition that views the person as social by nature and therefore called to community. Catholic teaching maintains that the person as cre-

68. Pope Francis, Homily during his visit to Lampedusa (July 8, 2013), at http://www.vatican.va/content/francesco/en/homilies/2013/documents/papa-francesco_20130708_omelia-lampedusa.html.

ated in the image and likeness of a triune God expresses their dignity through relationship. What Francis describes here as a "globalization of indifference" speaks to a denial of our human interdependence, a barrier to solidarity. He builds upon Benedict XVI's call to solidarity to counteract globalizing tendencies that emphasize profit over people in *Caritas in Veritate*. Unlike Benedict's highly rational appeal to embrace gratuitousness over competition and greed, Francis's challenge is emotional and evocative. He wants people to encounter the suffering engendered by social and economic systems that exclude. He wants humanity to weep.

Megan Clark points out how Francis builds upon the understanding within Catholic social thought of solidarity as a virtue, something that must be developed through practice. John Paul II and Benedict XVI developed the theological foundation of solidarity by pointing to ways human unity in relationship reflects the nature of the triune God. Clark observes a distinctive way that Francis understands solidarity—not only in Trinitarian terms but through the theology of the incarnation. Francis develops this in two ways; first, through Jesus's closeness to humanity as a model of solidarity and second, by reflecting on the encounter with Christ through solidarity with the impoverished.[69]

He does this in a unique way, Clark argues, by placing himself in relationship with them to amplify their visibility and agency. In doing so, he models an incarnational solidarity rooted in proximity with the excluded:

> Francis speaks directly to persons experiencing structural and systematic marginalization and exclusion, aware that the rest of the world is listening and watching. Using both his physical location and his words, he highlights the challenge of the very word solidarity through the dynamic of seeking comfort and trying to avoid the discomfort of facing injustice and calls for a conversion on the part of those observers remaining at a safe distance.[70]

---

69. Meghan J. Clark, "Pope Francis and the Christological Dimensions of Solidarity in Catholic Social Teaching," *Theological Studies* 80, no. 1 (March 2019): 102–22.

70. Clark, "Pope Francis," 115.

Francis argues that solidarity is an "uncomfortable word."[71] For him, solidarity is not about "different forms of welfare"[72] but building structures that enable the marginalized to participate in the common good. Francis's understanding of solidarity in the context of private property illustrates why it is an uncomfortable concept in light of neoliberal thinking:

> Solidarity is a spontaneous reaction by those who recognize that the social function of property and the universal destination of goods are realities which come before private property. The private ownership of goods is justified by the need to protect and increase them, so that they can better serve the common good; for this reason, solidarity must be lived as the decision to restore to the poor what belongs to them.[73]

This statement reflects Francis's formation in liberation theology, which places the preferential option for the poor at the center of the church's thought, and more importantly, action. Juan Carlos Scannone, SJ, has contributed to a growing body of literature analyzing the theological, historical, and cultural roots of Francis's thought. He points out that Francis's vision of a poor church for the poor reflects his pastoral experience and theological formation in a context shaped by liberation theology. While there is considerable consistency in various expressions of liberation theology, all revolving around the preferential option for the poor as a theological category with social, political, and economic implications, there are diverse expressions of liberation theology as it has emerged in multiple levels in the church and in a variety of Latin American contexts. Scannone describes the influence of the Argentine school of thought, theology of the people, as a particular strand of liberation theology which has influenced Pope Francis.[74]

---

71. Pope Francis, "Message for World Food Day," October 16, 2013.

72. Pope Francis, "Message for World Food Day."

73. EG, 189.

74. Juan Carlos Scannone, "Pope Francis and the Theology of the People," *Theological Studies* 77, no. 1 (March 2016): 118–35.

The theology of the people embraces historical and cultural analysis, in addition to social and economic analysis typical of liberation theology. Scannone argues that the cultural focus of the theology of the people is not understood as a substitute for structural analysis, but it also goes beyond Marxist categories to understand the realities of poverty. This focus can be observed in Francis's pastoral emphasis, his understanding of the *sensus fidei* and popular religiosity.[75] In *Evangelii Gaudium*, Francis describes the epistemological privilege of the poor as recipients of the Gospel. They are not passive recipients of the Gospel but agents of evangelization. "This is why I want a Church which is poor and for the poor. They have much to teach us. Not only do they share in the *sensus fidei*, but in their difficulties they know the suffering Christ. We need to let ourselves be evangelized by them."[76]

Beyond identifying the poor as evangelizers of the church, Francis recognizes the agency of the marginalized themselves as the sources of social transformation. In his address to the World Gathering of Popular Movements 2015 Bolivia, he said, "You, dear brothers and sisters, often work on little things, in local situations, amid forms of injustice which you do not simply accept but actively resist, standing up to an idolatrous system which excludes, debases, and kills."[77] He identified with the poor when he spoke of the deep knowledge of suffering and marginalization that motivates their resistance to the economy that kills:

> We are moved because "we have seen and heard" not a cold statistic but the pain of a suffering humanity, our own pain, our own flesh. This is something quite different than abstract theorizing or eloquent indignation. It moves us; it makes us attentive to others in an effort to move forward together.[78]

75. Scannone, "Pope Francis."

76. EG, 198.

77. Pope Francis, "Address to the Second World Meeting of Popular Movements," Bolivia (July 9, 2015), at http://www.vatican.va/content/francesco/en/speeches/2015/july/documents/papa-francesco_20150709_bolivia-movimenti-popolari.html.

78. Pope Francis, "Address to the Second World Meeting of Popular Movements."

The solidarity Francis envisions grows from the bottom up—from the poor and those who are close to the poor who are moved because they know the reality of suffering. Francis knows the poor because of sustained encounters with those living in poverty during his time as a pastor and as archbishop of Buenos Aires.[79] Francis stayed close to those living on the margins of society, regularly visiting impoverished neighborhoods and informal settlements, encouraging Jesuits in formation to do the same. He has encouraged bishops and priests to follow this example. As pope, he instructs clergy to be close to the people they lead. Pastors should smell of their sheep. This is consistent with his ecclesial vision of field hospital that prioritizes closeness, proximity, and being willing to be moved by suffering.

Field Hospital Ecclesiology

The spatial dynamics that frame Francis's social teaching give insight into his field hospital ecclesiology. The church is mobile and outward facing so it can enter into the messiness of the world, toward the peripheries where the wounds are most pressing. Francis makes clear that the church loses its ecclesial quality when it becomes self-referential:

> I want the Church to go out into the streets, I want us to defend ourselves against all worldliness, opposition to progress, from that which is comfortable, from that which is clericalism, from all that which means being closed up in ourselves. Parishes, schools, institutions are made in order to come out—if they do not do this, they become a non-governmental organization, and the Church must not be an NGO.[80]

79. Riccardi, *To the Margins.*

80. Pope Francis address on the Occasion of the XXVIII World Youth Day, Rio de Janeiro (July 25, 2013), at http://www.vatican.va/content/francesco/en/speeches /2013/july/documents/papa-francesco_20130725_gmg-argentini-rio.html.

At the same time, the church holds a space like a "mother with an open heart."[81] The church is open, its boundaries porous, so it can welcome people into its space. "The Church is called to be the house of the Father, with doors always wide open. One concrete sign of such openness is that our church doors should always be open, so that if someone, moved by the Spirit, comes there looking for God, he or she will not find a closed door."[82] Francis's call for open doors is both symbolic and concrete. He uses the metaphor of a merciful mother to urge the church to "slow down," "listen," and be a "place for everyone, with all their problems."[83] Yet, just as Francis's social teaching is always grounded in the concrete, material reality of poverty, his ecclesiology is grounded in concrete expressions of church. He envisions the church with actual open doors—welcoming the refugee, the unhoused, the disenfranchised into the space. These dynamics make the field hospital church that Francis puts forth uniquely poised to offer sanctuary. I focus on four dimensions of Francis's field hospital ecclesiology, each of which construct aspects of a theology of sanctuary: prophetic witness, embodied solidarity, sacramental praxis, and radical hospitality.

Prophetic Witness

Francis's theology of the church is rooted in his approach to evangelization laid out in *Evangelii Gaudium*. Central to his vision of a church that goes forth, he calls upon Christians to manifest the joy of the Gospel in the midst of a culture marked by consumerism and self-interest.[84] This must be rooted in and sustained by encounter with Christ, which fills the entire church with "missionary joy."[85] Francis differentiates evangelization from proselytizing, emphasizing "attractive witness" of the whole church as a testament to the Gospel.[86]

81. EG, 46–49.
82. EG, 47.
83. EG, 47.
84. EG, 2.
85. EG, 21.
86. EG, 14, 99.

Francis models this approach by prioritizing merciful action over doctrinal certitude and rational argumentation. Thomas Massaro suggests that Francis's "personal mark" on Catholic theology and social teaching is his emphasis on "material realities and physical human needs," reflecting an incarnational theology that runs counter to a "fixation on the purely rational."[87] Returning to Francis's homily at Lampedusa—he models the solidarity he proclaims through his physical proximity to suffering bodies. He denounces unjust immigration practices that serve countries with economic power, not through rational argumentation alone, but through a biblical narrative and emotional appeal to our common humanity.

Living out the Gospel narrative in concrete, public ways allows the church to challenge a throw-away culture and exercise a political voice without being directly engaged in politics. Francis resists an excessive privatization of religion in a way that is consonant with a secular age as one marked by multiple ways of relating to faith.[88] Instead of relying on the translation of religious claims into accessible public discourse, the field hospital church relies on the mode of witness, living into its particular narrative as an alternative to the status quo.

Embodied Solidarity

Since becoming pope, Francis has made ecclesial reform a priority. Francis's concern for internal aspects of the church—the church *ad intra*—does not contradict his insistence upon an outward focus on the church's mission—the church *ad extra*. Reforming the church is connected to prophetic witness because Francis recognizes that the church cannot speak with credibility unless it embodies the solidarity it proclaims. He has challenged the culture of the Roman Curia with efforts toward greater transparency and accountability.[89] He has

87. Massaro, "Pope Francis on Overcoming Exclusion," 871.

88. Charles Taylor, *A Secular Age*, Gifford Lectures (Cambridge, MA: Harvard University Press, 2007).

89. Massimo Faggioli, *Pope Francis: Tradition in Transition* (Mahwah, NJ: Paulist Press, 2015).

denounced clericalism, instructing pastors to be close to the people, to smell of the sheep.[90]

Francis's inclusive call to witness to the power of the Gospel emphasizes the church as the people of God, an image elevated by the Second Vatican Council. Conceiving of the church in this way emphasizes the common call to participate in Christ's ministry by virtue of baptism and considers all particular vocations as flowing from this sacrament. From this ecclesiology, Francis has put forth a theology of ministry that challenges clericalism in all forms, emphasizes episcopal collegiality over centralization of magisterial authority, and elevates the laity as leaven and light, gifted with a sense of the faith, *sensus fidelium*, that allows them to "discern what is of God."[91]

Sacramental Praxis

Related to Francis's recognition of the sense of the faithful is his appreciation for popular religion, which Cecilia Gonzalez-Andrieu describes as "human creativity in search of an encounter with the divine."[92] It is in his attention to "uniqueness, embodiment, and relationality"[93]—central aspects of popular religion—that allows Francis to affirm unity in diversity as pastor of a global, multicultural church. In *Evangelii Gaudium*, Francis discusses the "evangelizing power of popular piety" representing the "never-ending process of inculturation"[94] that allows the church to be a sacrament of salvation for everyone.[95]

Attention to the dignity of culture expressed in the daily lives of ordinary people informs Francis's ecclesiology. For Francis, formed

---

90. Pope Francis, Homily on Holy Thursday (March 28, 2013), at http://www.vatican.va/content/francesco/es/homilies/2013/documents/papa-francesco_20130328_messa-crismale.html.

91. EG, 119.

92. Cecilia Gonzalez-Andrieu, "Evangelization, Inculturation, and Popular Religion," in *Go into the Streets! The Welcoming Church of Pope Francis*, ed. Richard Gaillardetz and Thomas Rausch (Mahwah, NJ: Paulist Press, 2016), 35.

93. Gonzalez-Andrieu, "Evangelization, Inculturation, and Popular Religion," 33.

94. EG, 126.

95. EG, 112.

by the theology of the people, a poor church for the poor embraces the ways God is revealed through concrete practices of faith as sacramental. These practices of faith, especially among the poor, reveal the beauty of the Gospel in the midst of suffering and paradox.[96] Popular religion, as an expression of creativity and cultural particularity, is an aesthetic practice.[97]

Stan Chu Ilo emphasizes the aesthetic dimension of Francis's ecclesiology as well. "Pope Francis shows through his theological aesthetics that the church's identity and mission can be recovered fully only if the church becomes a seeing eye, showing the beautiful Christian way in the contradictions of history."[98] Ilo embraces the image of the church as a sacrament, emphasizing the role of the poor in facilitating a transformative encounter with Christ in history. He describes Francis's "illuminative ecclesiology" as the "form of witnessing and proclamation that can be experienced as a transformative encounter with the Lord Jesus Christ by all—Christians and non-Christians—through the priorities and practices of the church."[99]

Radical Hospitality

Mercy provides a unifying thread throughout Francis's theological reflection on the church. Salvation, of which the entire evangelizing church is to be a sign, is "a work of [God's] mercy,"[100] not of human efforts. Mercy shines through the people of God when they participate in creating a culture of encounter and closeness, especially to the poor. Francis uses the language of accompaniment to speak to this task. "In our world, ordained ministers and other pastoral workers can make present the fragrance of Christ's closeness and his personal gaze. The Church will have to initiate everyone—priests, religious and

---

96. EG, 42.

97. Gonzalez-Andrieu, "Evangelization, Inculturation, and Popular Religion."

98. Stan Chu Ilo, *A Poor and Merciful Church: The Illuminative Ecclesiology of Pope Francis* (Maryknoll, NY: Orbis, 2018), 36.

99. Ilo, *A Poor and Merciful Church,* 29.

100. EG, 112.

laity—into this 'art of accompaniment' which teaches us to remove our sandals before the sacred ground of the other (cf. *Ex* 3:5)."[101] In this regard, ministers model the way God accompanies those who suffer:

> To those who suffer, God does not provide arguments which explain everything; rather, his response is that of an accompanying presence, a history of goodness which touches every story of suffering and opens up a ray of light. In Christ, God himself wishes to share this path with us and to offer us his gaze so that we might see the light within it (Heb 12:2).[102]

Kate Ward relates Francis's understanding of accompaniment to hospitality.[103] She argues, following James Keenan, that the Jesuit approach to hospitality is best understood as walking with others in the world. This approach to hospitality differs from the more well-known version exemplified by the Benedictine practice of welcoming the other into one's dwelling place. Hospitality as accompaniment resonates well with the image of a field hospital church, which goes outward to meet people where they are, bringing mercy to the world's greatest needs.

Francis demonstrates a keen awareness that sometimes a welcoming space is the greatest need in his practical gestures of solidarity, including creating physical spaces for refugees and unhoused people and challenging all churches to do the same. This concrete practice of space-sharing has been part of sanctuary throughout history and in a context like San Francisco, where space is a commodity that few can afford, perhaps it is the most prophetic form of sanctuary. Consonant with Francis's robust critique of neoliberalism, such practices of space-sharing resist the absolutizing of private property.

---

101. EG, 169.

102. Pope Francis, Encyclical on Faith, *Lumen Fidei* (June 29, 2013), 57.

103. Kate Ward, "Jesuit and Feminist Hospitality: Pope Francis' Virtue Response to Inequality," *Religions* 8, no. 4 (2017): 71, https://doi.org/10.3390/rel8040071.

Time Is Greater than Space?

With Francis's focus on the material realities of suffering, his incarnational approach to solidarity, and integration of spatial metaphors into Catholic social thought, one might be surprised by his insistence on the priority of time over space. In *Evangelii Gaudium*, Francis lays out four principles that "derive from the pillars of the Church's social doctrine" and are "related to the constant tensions present in every social reality"[104] to guide the application of Catholic social thought. Scholars have highlighted these hermeneutical keys for understanding the roots of Francis's thought and his unique contribution to Catholic social thought: time is greater than space, unity prevails over conflict, realities are more important than ideas, the whole is greater than the part.

Francis views these tensions in social life dialectically, reflecting the thought of German theologian Romano Guardini. Guardini offers an alternative to Hegelian dialectical thought by arguing that unity is not achieved through the annihilation of difference but through creative tension of parts within the whole. Guardini's emphasis on unity in diversity influenced Francis's vision of dialogue, which undergirds his critique of colonization and globalization that attacks the dignity of difference.[105]

Understood within this framework, Francis's assertion of time over space relates to his critique of hegemonic structures that dominate and suppress difference. In *Evangelii Gaudium*, he presents time and space within the tension between fullness and limitation. "Fullness evokes the desire for complete possession, while limitation is a wall set before us."[106] Francis sees a problematic emphasis on space in the desire to conquer and possess. This is represented in the impulse toward colonization. In contrast, "giving priority to time means being concerned

---

104. EG, 221.

105. Joseph Flipper, "The Time of Encounter in the Political Theology of Pope Francis," in *Pope Francis and the Event of Encounter*, ed. John Cavadini and Donald Wallenfang, Global Perspectives on the New Evangelization (Eugene, OR: Pickwick Publications, 2018), 119–32.

106. EG, 222.

about initiating processes rather than possessing spaces."[107] Elsewhere, Francis associates time with openness and process and space with the consolidation of power. In *Amoris Laetitia*, he evokes the principle to caution parents against excessive control over one's children that does not allow them to recognize where they are on a journey toward maturity.[108] In *Laudato Si*, he reminds the reader that "time is greater than space" to encourage the initiation of processes to address the environmental crisis which are hindered by "myopic" consolidation of political power.[109]

Francis's emphasis on time does not imply that space is not important. Rather, he insists on the dialectical relationship between time and space, critiquing approaches to space that elevate fullness over limitation. Scannone argues that Francis "does not ignore the question of space but looks at it rather from a temporal perspective."[110] Before he became pope, Bergoglio expressed concern over a postmodern sense of space divorced from collective memory. He described urban spaces governed by utility as "no-spaces," divorced from culture and identity, they are spatially rootless.[111] A forgetfulness of time and collective memory is connected to a lack of hope. In *Fratelli Tutti*, Francis expresses particular concern for young people who are distracted by technology and consumerism, becoming shallow without regard to tradition. He argues that the forgetfulness of history opens the door to "cultural colonization"—when the ideals of democracy, freedom, and justice are subverted to incite violence and polarization.[112]

Time is a central category in political theology and liberation theology, which emphasize God's liberating activity in history. Political theologian Johann Baptist Metz argued that Christianity had become

---

107. EG, 223.

108. Pope Francis, Post-Synodal Exhortation on the Family, The Joy of Love, *Amoris Laetitia* (March 19, 2016), 261.

109. Pope Francis, Encyclical on the Care for our Common Home, *Laudato Si* (May 24, 2015), 178.

110. Scannone, "Pope Francis and the Theology of the People," 128–9.

111. Flipper, "The Time of Encounter," 123.

112. FT, 13–14.

a bourgeois religion because it forgot the prophetic roots of its own history. By retrieving the dangerous memory of Christ's suffering and overcoming violence, the church exercises solidarity with those who struggle for justice. Liberation theologian Gustavo Gutierrez challenged an individual ahistorical view of salvation in favor of an understanding of God who labors in history to liberate those who suffer oppression. Francis has said:

> We must not focus on occupying the spaces where power is exercised, but rather on starting long-run historical processes. We must initiate processes rather than occupy spaces. God manifests himself in time and is present in the processes of history. This gives priority to actions that give birth to new historical dynamics. And it requires patience, waiting.[113]

Francis's own Ignatian spirituality emphasizes the encounter with God in time through discernment. Jesuits and other practitioners of Ignatian spirituality maintain that God operates in the inner dynamics of a person and the unfolding processes of one's experiences. Rooted in the conviction that God can be discovered in all things, this spirituality prioritizes reality and resists a withdrawal from the material world. Considering Francis's theological, philosophical, and spiritual commitments, his emphasis on time over space does not contradict his emphasis on the physical world, embodiment, and geographical metaphors.

However, there are limits to Francis's dialectical thinking when it comes to articulating an ecclesiology of sanctuary. In this book, I observe how sanctuary spaces are constructed through concrete practices such as those that Francis embraces—housing refugees in churches, transforming Vatican buildings into homeless shelters. When space is conceived in opposition to process, the dynamic processes that in fact construct spaces can be overlooked. Postmodern and postcolonial conceptions of power as interwoven with resistance lend themselves

---

113. Pope Francis, "A Big Heart Open to God."

to a more complex understanding of space than Francis's dialectical method captures.[114]

Guided by the conviction that the church must bear witness to the justice it proclaims within its own structures, Francis has undertaken a process of reforming the church. While this reform includes sharing power with women by creating opportunities for them to exercise authority as laypeople, it does not include a reimagining of formal leadership reserved for ordained men. While the church itself is conceived in feminine terms in Francis's preferred metaphor of the church as a mother, gender roles are understood within the same dialectical structure that animates Francis's thought. The framework of gender complementarity justifies the exclusion of women from formal representation of the church, while motherhood is elevated as an abstract, disembodied model of the church.[115] This structure of ministry not only impacts gender relations in the church, it impacts the church's ability to embody solidarity in sanctuary.

This chapter has explored the social teaching and ecclesiology of Pope Francis, highlighting the field hospital church that goes out to the margins and holds space for the disenfranchised. The key dimensions of Francis's ecclesiology—prophetic witness, embodied solidarity, sacramental praxis, and radical hospitality—begin to construct a theology of sanctuary. Yet as we explore ideas, it is worth noting that for Francis, reality takes precedence over ideas. Practices of sanctuary in San Francisco deepen engagement with Francis's field hospital ecclesiology.

---

114. This book will draw upon the spatial turn in philosophy and theology, represented in the postmodern philosophy by Michel Foucault and Henri de Lefebvre and in theology by constructivist approaches to sacred space in the thought of Kim Knott (*The Location of Religion: A Spatial Analysis* [London: Routledge, 2005]); Jonathan Z. Smith (*To Take Place: Toward Theory in Ritual* [Chicago: Chicago University Press, 1987]); and Catherine Bell (*Ritual Theory, Ritual Practice* [Oxford: Oxford University Press, 1992]).

115. Tina Beattie, "Transforming Time: The Maternal Church and the Pilgrimage of Faith," in *Pope Francis, Evangelii Gaudium, and the Renewal of the Church*, ed. Duncan Dormor and Alana Harris (Mahwah, NJ: Paulist Press, 2017).

Chapter 2

Sanctuary as Prophetic Witness

At a busy intersection of San Francisco's Mission District, an interfaith group of nearly fifty people gathered to observe Ash Wednesday with a ritual of repentance. Standing around a small bonfire at a popular commuter train station, faith leaders took turns naming and burning collective sins of our nation—homophobia, xenophobia, racism. The ritual spoke to the Christian theological conviction that humanity has gone astray and that we need to seek forgiveness and reorient ourselves toward God. However, this traditional religious practice did not take place in a church but rather a public square in a largely secular city.

The ritual marked two moments in time—one guided by the liturgical calendar of the Christian faith and the other situated in the political history of the United States. This day in March was the first Ash Wednesday following the inauguration of President Donald Trump. Trump, who ran on an anti-immigrant platform, had already issued a series of executive orders aimed at heightening border security and limiting immigration from certain countries.[1] This mobilized faith

---

1. Donald Trump issued three controversial executive orders in January and March 2017 related to immigration: "Enhancing Public Safety in the Interior of the United

communities like St. John the Evangelist to issue a public declaration of sanctuary.

In addition to the timing of the ritual, the space holds significance. Carrying signs indicating solidarity with immigrants and resistance to xenophobia, the interfaith group processed from the train station to St. John the Evangelist. Walking through the Mission District, a predominantly Latinx neighborhood undergoing rapid gentrification, we are met with curious stares, waves, and smiles of support. When we arrive at the door of St. John the Evangelist, intentionally painted red to signal their affinity with the historical practice of sanctuary, a media crew gathers around the pastor while he reads a public declaration of sanctuary.

The public quality of the statement is significant for many people involved in the New Sanctuary Movement. St. John's had been practicing sanctuary for several years. They were involved in the sanctuary movement of the 1980s and have continued this commitment in partnership with a local nonprofit, the Central American Resource Center (CARECEN), providing accompaniment and advocacy for immigrants and the Latinx community of San Francisco. St. John's sanctuary commitment extends beyond justice for immigrants. The church sees itself as a sanctuary to the LGBTQ community, especially when they were ostracized during the AIDS crisis of the 1980s. And St. John's is one of two congregations in San Francisco to partner with the Gubbio Project, a nonprofit organization that creates sanctuary for unhoused people by welcoming them to sleep in worship spaces. By choosing this particular time and space to issue a public declaration of sanctuary, St. John's is asserting their religious identity in the public sphere.

This chapter addresses two questions that emerge among San Francisco sanctuary congregations like St. John the Evangelist, who are participating in and shaping the New Sanctuary Movement. First,

---

States" (January 25, 2017); "Border Security and Immigration Enforcement Improvements" (January 25, 2017); and "Protecting the Nation from Foreign Terrorist Entry into the United States" (March 6, 2017), at https://www.whitehouse.gov/presidential-actions.

should the church engage in politics? While the majority of sanctuary leaders I interviewed represented congregations that were supportive of practicing sanctuary, some tensions emerged over the public declaration. The debates surrounding the decision to declare sanctuary reveal theological differences related to the nature of the church and the church's relationships to society and politics. Highlighting conceptions of the public sphere that challenge the liberal tradition, I consider sanctuary to be an alternative public space for a reconceptualization of ecclesial and political identity.

The second question this chapter will address is, *how* should the church engage in politics? In other words, can particular faith claims carry relevance outside the tradition that generated them? Can faith communities dialogue with a wider public without losing the critical, prophetic dimension of their claims? These challenges reflect key debates in public theology, and sanctuary movements provide an important context to reflect on these debates. Public declarations of sanctuary both draw upon and disrupt liberal political theory, inviting us to consider the nature of religious claims beyond rigid conceptions of public reason. Sanctuary demonstrates that the rational translation of religious claims is not sufficient for prophetic action. Following feminist critical theorists who have challenged the idea that there is a single, inclusive public sphere governed by reason, I will highlight how sanctuary leaders have used performance, testimony, and narrative to articulate a political theology.

I draw upon the political theologies of William Cavanaugh and Johann Baptist Metz in conversation with Pope Francis to construct an ecclesiology of prophetic witness in the face of neoliberalism and related structural injustices. Prophetic witness is a central feature of Francis's field hospital church. His vision of the church flows from the conviction that "An authentic faith—which is never comfortable or completely personal—always involves a deep desire to change the world, to transmit values, to leave this earth somehow better that we found it."[2] He envisions a church that goes forth into the world and

2. EG, 183.

witnesses to the transformative joy of the Gospel, rejecting the privatization of faith while also recognizing the legitimacy of a pluralistic public sphere.

Cavanaugh and Metz approach the relationship between the church and politics differently, resulting in helpful mutual criticisms in their ecclesiologies. Cavanaugh, who argues for a form of Christian anarchism in the tradition of Stanley Hauerwas, regards the church as an alternative political body, marked by political practices in contrast to the practices of the state. Metz accepts the distinction between church and politics but argues that the church must exercise a sociopolitical function as a bearer of dangerous memory of those who suffer and are vindicated by God in history. They both articulate political theology as the antidote to the excessive privatization of religion and the church's modern acquiescence to the Enlightenment model of human progress (Metz) and the excesses of neoliberal capitalism (Cavanaugh).

Sanctuary as prophetic witness goes beyond the translation of faith to continually disrupt the limitations in the sanctuary movement itself. Through symbolic and liturgical political practices, some churches not only enter a neutral public sphere, they contest the assumed duality of public/private, religious/secular. The critical dimension of sanctuary aims not only to transform the politics of the state but also to transform the identity and practices of the church. Interviews and observations reveal two dynamics—an outward movement that resists the privatization of religion and an inward movement in which churches reread their own histories in light of their sanctuary commitment.

Sanctuary and Public Theology

Religion in the Public Sphere

When I began interviewing participants in the San Francisco sanctuary movement, I anticipated the greatest barrier to participating in sanctuary to be the fear of breaking the law. This fear was not absent; however, talking to people whose congregations were divided on the practice of sanctuary revealed another concern. Organizers and leaders around sanctuary identified as a barrier the fear that the congregation would be seen as too political. Behind this concern is a particular theology of the church, assumptions that frame the relationship between the church and the world, more specifically, the church and the public sphere. These assumptions, often implicit, reflect cultural beliefs about the relationship between religion and the state.

A widespread feature of US church-state culture reflects a liberal philosophical tradition that differentiates the public sphere of political engagement from the private sphere of religious belief. The roots of this tradition go back to the seventeenth century when religious wars threatened the stability of Western Europe. Modern liberal political theory responds to the potential divisiveness of religion in a pluralistic context by elevating reasonable discourse as the mode for negotiating common interests. Representing this view, John Rawls has argued that the comprehensive doctrines offered by religion cannot achieve the kind of overlapping consensus necessary for a pluralistic society to pursue the common good. In his earlier work, Rawls argued that religious citizens must bracket their faith claims to deliberate on public interests. He later conceded that religious claims had a place in public deliberation only if they could also be justified by generally accessible, reasonable arguments.[3]

Like Rawls, Jürgen Habermas embraces the premise that religious claims must be translated into rational arguments as the proper mode for public discourse. Habermas further accepts the possibility that the religious person does not have to bracket the convictions of faith prior to entering public debate. What Habermas adds to Rawls's view is that the process of translation is a mutual responsibility of religious and nonreligious citizens. Although Habermas does not regard religious claims as such to be generalizable, he recognizes their unique value in society. Therefore, the nonreligious counterpart should approach

3. John Rawls, *Political Liberalism* (New York: Columbia University Press, 2005).

religious claims with an openness and willingness to participate in the translation process.[4]

Jeffrey Stout challenges the premise that religious claims must be translated by questioning some of the foundational assumptions of the liberal tradition. First, he points out that the liberal nation-state is not neutral but guided by a set of values and beliefs, including the assumption that tolerance involves bracketing off one's particular religious beliefs in public discourse. Against Richard Rorty's accusation that religion is a conversation stopper, he differentiates between religious claims, expressed in a variety of ways, and faith claims, which tend not to offer justifications for their commitments.[5] He also notes that nonreligious people make claims on the basis of faith that could equally be described as conversation stoppers. Second, he argues that religious pluralism, like any pluralism, should not be treated like a threat to unity. He rejects Rawls's assumption that translating religious principles into rational arguments is a sign of respect, arguing that "Real respect for others takes seriously the distinctive point of view each other occupies. It is respect for individuality, for difference."[6] Stout's theory follows his observation of the power of faith-based organizing, particularly in multifaith coalitions, to enact social change.[7]

The Limits of Translation
On one hand, the sanctuary movement represents the kind of exchange Habermas seems to be inviting. Sanctuary is a site of translation, where faith-based action is expressed in secular values and reasonable political norms. Sanctuary as a concept functions meaningfully in religious and

---

4. See Jürgen Habermas, *Religion and Rationality* (Cambridge: Polity Press, 2002); Jürgen Habermas, *Between Naturalism and Religion*, trans. Ciaran Cronin (Cambridge: Polity Press, 2008); Jürgen Habermas, *An Awareness of What is Missing*, trans. Ciaran Cronin (Cambridge: Polity Press, 2010).

5. Jeffrey Stout, *Democracy and Tradition* (Princeton: Princeton University Press, 2004).

6. Stout, *Democracy and Tradition*, 73.

7. Jeffrey Stout. *Blessed Are the Organized Grassroots: Democracy in America* (Princeton: Princeton University Press, 2010).

nonreligious settings and fosters collaboration among faith communities and secular entities advocating for immigrants. A local example proves the significance of faith communities in ushering in a broader sanctuary commitment reflected in municipal practice and cultural attitudes. Peter Mancina details the crucial role of faith communities in motivating city officials toward a pro-immigrant stance and eventually to enact a sanctuary ordinance in San Francisco. Faith leaders provided an ethical rationale for sanctuary that was both rooted in the particularities of their tradition and articulated to correspond to the espoused progressive values of the city.[8] So the biblical mandate to love one's neighbor was translated into a San Franciscan ethos that celebrates diversity and strives toward inclusion.

On a broader scope, Latin American liberation theology[9] informed the US sanctuary movement in the 1980s, leading to transnational solidarity that provided the basis for a critique of the US government. This faith-driven solidarity eventually contributed to the US government providing Temporary Protected Status (TPS) for Central American refugees. In her study of the 1980s sanctuary movement, Susan Bibler Coutin documents the impact of liberation theology, noting that it

8. Peter Mancina, "The Birth of a Sanctuary-City: A History of Governmental Sanctuary in San Francisco" in *Sanctuary Practices in International Perspectives: Migration, Citizenship, and Social Movements*, ed. Randy Lippert and Sean Rehagg (London: Routledge, 2013).

9. Interpreting the Christian faith from the perspective of the poor and oppressed, liberation theology emerged on multiple levels of the church in Latin America during the late 1960s through '80s. It was developed by Christian base communities whose reading of Scripture was accompanied by consciousness-raising of structural injustices, theologically identified as social sins. It was articulated by academically trained theologians who drew upon Marxist tools for social analysis coupled with the preferential option for the poor as the guiding hermeneutic to the Christian faith. And it was endorsed by Latin American bishops such as Oscar Romero and Episcopal Conference of Latin America (CELAM) gathered at Medellin (1968) and Puebla (1979), representing a shift away from the church's historical alliance with the politically and economically powerful. For an overview of key voices and themes in liberation theology, see *The Cambridge Companion to Liberation Theology*, ed. Christopher Rowland (Cambridge, UK: Cambridge University Press, 2007).

provided a theological mandate for solidarity with Central American refugees and migrants. She names a "quasi-sacred reality of the Central American poor" that drew North American sanctuary workers into relationship with them. This experience of solidarity provided the basis to critique the United States' political and economic relationship to Central America.[10]

On the other hand, the history of sanctuary points out the limitations of translation. Gary Slater points out that while definitions of sanctuary vary among municipalities to some degree, the "baseline" approach to sanctuary means noncooperation with federal immigration authorities. This does not necessarily evoke the kind of solidarity rooted in liberation theology. He suggests that sanctuary creates an ethically neutral space that should be filled by sanctuary activists:

> The upshot of the legal/ethical distinction with respect to sanctuary cities is that of an ethically negative space at the local level, one that can be filled with various forms of religious life in light of turning strangers into neighbors. An ethics of sanctuary cities can build on this necessary but insufficient set of policies to articulate a more robust vision for the fulfillment of sanctuary's potential.[11]

The sanctuary practice of noninterference may be a reasonable baseline for municipal expressions. However, it fails to capture the theological dimensions of sanctuary as a prophetic practice of hospitality that disrupts the very notion of private property by welcoming the refugee, unhoused, or persecuted person into a shared space. The emphasis on tolerance and noninterference follows a liberal conception of human rights but fails to embody the positive notion of human rights enshrined in Catholic social thought. Pope Francis observes a disconnect between countries who claim universal human rights but

---

10. Susan Bibler Coutin, *The Culture of Protest: Religious Activism and the U.S. Sanctuary Movement* (Boulder: Westview Press, 1993), 59.

11. Gary Slater, "From Strangers to Neighbors: Toward an Ethics of Sanctuary Cities," *Journal of Moral Theology* 7, no. 2 (2018): 57–85, at 60.

do not provide the conditions for everyone to realize their rights. He connects the unequal recognition of rights to "reductive anthropological visions" which prioritizes profits over people.[12] Immigration policy informed by Catholic social thought must go beyond granting migrants a measure of civic rights to ensure their full participation in the common good through access to basic needs, such as housing, as well as access to the means of full integral development as persons in community.

Some argue that the current sanctuary movement, both in its religious and nonreligious expressions, fails to go far enough in dismantling structures that oppress not only immigrants but other groups—that is, people who are unhoused, impoverished, or incarcerated. Naomi Paik argues that the current sanctuary movement relies on liberal frameworks that legitimize the power of the state, rendering the movement ultimately ineffective. By failing to address the systemic criminalization of communities of color and corresponding neoliberal interests made concrete in the privatization of prisons, the sanctuary movement fails to promote the kind of solidarity and inclusion it proclaims. Paik is particularly critical of the power religious congregations have exerted in deciding who gets sanctuary and who is excluded.[13] By separating immigrants into categories marked by those deserving of sanctuary and those who are not, Yukich argues that sanctuary participants play a role in fueling the rhetoric of good versus bad immigrant.[14] Paik argues that "the future of the sanctuary movement must fight for all oppressed peoples" and finds the most compelling expressions of sanctuary to be ones that recognize intersecting forms of oppression and resist the neoliberal interests that benefit from them.[15]

12. FT, 22.

13. Naomi Paik, "Abolitionist Futures and the US Sanctuary Movement," *Race and Class* 59, no. 2 (October 2017): 3–25, at 14.

14. Grace Yukich, "Constructing the Model Immigrant: Movement Strategy and Immigrant Deservingness in the New Sanctuary Movement," *Social Problems* 60, no. 3 (2013): 302–20.

15. Paik, "Abolitionist Futures," 18. One example of this is the Freedom Cities Movement, which takes an explicitly intersectional approach to community safety.

Interfaith coalitions that support sanctuary in San Francisco provide a mechanism for self-critique and are addressing some of Paik's concerns. For example, the Interfaith Movement for Human Integrity (IM4HI), one of the primary coalitions for faith-based immigration advocacy, has explicitly connected their campaign to end mass incarceration and systemic racism through criminalization into their sanctuary stance. The work of IM4HI provides a faith-based rationale for sanctuary congregations to embrace immigrants who fall outside of the national and municipal discourse around who deserves compassion.[16]

The work of IM4HI demonstrates that faith communities have a key role in ushering in a prophetic form of sanctuary that disrupts power structures that benefit the interests of few. To harness the resources of faith, however, progressive religious groups must overcome the internal and external perception that tolerance and explicit religious claims are incompatible. Echoing Stout, the problem is not secularization or religious pluralism. It has more to do with the false assumption that tolerance or respect requires bracketing religious particularity. The liberal notion of the public sphere and rational discourse fail to account for the unique value of religious claims. Some post-Habermasian critical theorists provide a more adequate account that will later help us analyze the way faith communities articulate and enact a theology of sanctuary.

They recognize that police violence against Black people is interconnected to state-sanctioned violence against immigrants and advocate for safety for all marginalized people. Sanctuary represents one aspect of Freedom Cities' larger aim toward liberation from oppressive power exercised by corporations and the state. See https://freedomcities.org/.

16. The Interfaith Movement for Human Integrity describes its vision: "Working at the intersection of spirituality and social movements, we mobilize congregations to take a stand on issues of social justice like immigration and mass incarceration, and we engage people of faith to develop their own leadership so they can stand up against racism, discrimination, and the political challenges of the day. We bring a faith voice to social movement coalitions, providing a compassionate religious perspective amidst the clamor of angry political actors." See https://www.im4humanintegrity.org.

Rethinking the Public Voice of Religion

In her analysis of the sanctuary movement, Alicia Steinmetz suggests that the liberal conception of public reason fails to see the nature and meaning of religious claims in the movement. She argues that even the strictest Rawlsian account would include the religious rationale for sanctuary but that the limited notion of public reason obscures the kind of contribution religion made to the movement.[17] Within the context of postmodernity, which has challenged the ideal of reason as a universalizing mode of discourse, there is an opportunity to explore the unique value of religion in movements like sanctuary.

Feminist thinkers have pushed Habermasian critical theory in ways that are particularly helpful for developing a critical understanding of faith-based sanctuary. Breaking down the traditionally gendered separation of private versus public interests, feminist critical theory has challenged the notion that there is a single public sphere to which everyone has access. Exposing the ways in which historically marginalized groups have strategically navigated through exclusion to assert their interests as political concerns, feminists have illuminated alternative forms of public debate, ones that more adequately speak to the nature of religious discourse.

Habermas defines the public sphere as a place to negotiate shared interests through free speech and rational discourse. This concept is based on the premise of inclusive participation, which is fundamental to a successful democracy. Although he recognizes historical exclusions, Habermas maintains that the ideal of accessibility for everyone has functioned as a regulatory principle to promote inclusion.[18] Nancy Fraser points out the ways that historical exclusions have also functioned in society. She argues that groups subjugated by gender, race,

---

17. Alicia Steinmetz, "Sanctuary and the Limits of Public Reason: A Deweyan Corrective," *Politics and Religion* 11, no. 3 (2018): 498–521.

18. Jürgen Habermas, *The Structural Transformation of the Public Sphere: An Inquiry into a Category of Bourgeois Society*, trans. Thomas Burger (Cambridge, MA: MIT Press, 1989).

and class have created alternative publics, sometimes overlapping, sometimes competing, with the dominant public sphere.[19]

Iris Marion Young similarly problematizes the idea of inclusion. She theorizes two forms of exclusion from political participation. External exclusion is overt and includes unjust voter registration procedures or big lobby groups that exercise political power through financial power. Internal exclusion occurs among people who are formally included in the democratic process but marginalized or not taken seriously because of racism, sexism, or classism. Internal exclusion tends to limit the kinds of arguments that are regarded as appropriate for political engagement. Against the dominant definition of reasonable arguments, Young argues that there are multiple, legitimate ways to engage in public discourse, including greeting, rhetoric, and narrative.[20] Her discussion of narrative is particularly relevant to this context, given the role of storytelling in sanctuary. According to Young, storytelling can give voice to those who have been systematically excluded from public discourse, making visible their suffering. It can forge understanding across differences and facilitate political engagement among local affinities. It can communicate values and meaning as well as lead to the construction of new knowledge.[21] Maria Pia Lara has pointed out the role of narrative in creating counter-publics for subjugated groups to exercise political agency.[22]

In what follows, I examine how sanctuary congregations employ these strategies, particularly performance and narrative, to articulate a public theology. The theology represents an outward movement of political engagement and an inward movement of theological identity, blurring the distinction between the two. I will analyze these movements with three ecclesiological perspectives—those of William

19. Nancy Fraser, "Rethinking the Public Sphere: A Contribution to the Critique of Actually Existing Democracy," *Social Text* no. 25/26 (1990): 56–80.

20. Iris Marion Young, *Inclusion and Democracy* (Oxford: Oxford University Press, 2002), chapter 4.

21. Young, *Inclusion and Democracy*, 70–77.

22. Maria Pia Lara, *Moral Textures: Feminist Narratives in the Public Sphere* (Cambridge: Polity Press, 1998).

Cavanagh, Johann Baptist Metz, and Pope Francis. While these thinkers represent different approaches to political theology, they highlight important aspects of sanctuary both as a set of political practices and as a hermeneutic for reading the Christian narrative.

"We Had to Do Something"— Sanctuary and Political Identity

> After the election of Trump, everybody, including me, . . . were just reeling, and I'm really upset and determined to respond. It felt like a call as church to put what we say we believe into action more than ever. Like it was just a real wake-up call on so many levels. . . . We were becoming more aware about the state of our immigration laws and becoming more aware about what happens around detention and deportation. . . . We had to do something.[23]

When I asked members of sanctuary congregations about their motivation to make a public declaration of sanctuary, by far the most prevalent answer was political. Represented in the quote above, most leaders cited the 2016 election of Donald Trump as the impetus for declaring sanctuary. Many of these churches had been involved in immigration advocacy prior to 2016 but either did not use the word sanctuary to describe their practices or they did not feel compelled to make a public declaration. The political moment drew them into the public sphere, to declare sanctuary as a public witness to their identity and progressive values as Christians.

In her ethnographic work on the New Sanctuary Movement (NSM), Grace Yukich observes how faith communities negotiate their public identity through sanctuary. She describes the NSM as a multi-targeted social movement, aimed not only at immigration reform but also seeking to transform public perception of religion. Beyond their explicit political agenda, "It was also a group of mostly progressive

---

23. Interview with a sanctuary participant on August 21, 2018.

religious leaders and laypeople working for religious conversion and transformation, struggling for greater authority to define religion in a public sphere often dominated by conservative voices."[24]

I observed this among the congregations in this study as well. For most congregations, the public declaration emerged organically from their history and practices of inclusion and solidarity. These congregations had been involved in immigration advocacy or other concrete expressions of their progressive identity, marked by the values of tolerance, inclusion, and social justice. For other congregations, the process of discernment or the declaration of sanctuary sparked internal debates, surfacing political and theological tensions within the communities. Particularly when sanctuary was introduced as a response to Trump, congregations wrestled with the question of their proper place in politics as a Christian church.

One congregation offers a particularly striking example of how these debates ensued. The interviews present a church that is changing from a white, rich "social club" toward a politically engaged, diverse, inclusive church. The sanctuary declaration was situated within this shift in identity and pushed forward by leaders whose own nondominant identities were cited as a motivation to instigate the shift. Prior to declaring sanctuary, a group within the church became active in immigration advocacy and leadership participated in Faith in Action and the Interfaith Movement for Human Integrity. Being part of the larger sanctuary coalition was named as important as they articulated their identity as a sanctuary congregation. The decision to declare sanctuary went through the ecclesial process of decision-making, reflecting the congregational style of the church. It involved education around the meaning of sanctuary, including reassurance that it would not involve physical sanctuary or breaking the law. For this community, sanctuary reflected a commitment to pro-immigrant advocacy, accompaniment, and education about immigration as a social justice issue. Although the measure passed through a majority vote, the declaration of sanctuary

24. Grace Yukich, *One Family under God: Immigration Politics and Progressive Religion in America* (New York: Oxford University Press, 2013), 9.

in this context was controversial. Some people left and some people withheld financial contributions to the church in protest.

The congregation made visible their sanctuary commitment by hanging a large banner on the outer facade of the church. The banner, adopted by a number of sanctuary congregations, has an image of the Holy Family fleeing Herod and the words "Immigrants and Refugees Welcome Here." Next to the sanctuary banner, they displayed a rainbow flag and Black Lives Matter banner—all of which manifest the ecclesial identity of the church as one that is politically engaged and aligned with progressive values. Members of the congregation who disapproved of the banners cited a concern over being too political.

It is difficult to parse out political differences from theological differences, especially given the limitations of my data. I spoke to sanctuary supporters who highlighted internal debates from their perspectives. My focus shall remain on the sanctuary leaders and their theological strategies for addressing the differences. The crux of the issue, at least from the perspective of the sanctuary leaders, was not so much around differences in values or particular stances on immigration. Congregants even suggested that they practice sanctuary without making a public declaration. For them, the issue at stake was over-politicizing the Gospel. The leaders in this congregation countered this view with scriptural mandates to welcome the stranger and presented Jesus's message as one with political dimensions.

Those who opposed the sanctuary declaration in this congregation expressed the view that the church should not be involved in politics. One sanctuary leader described the opposition he encountered:

> They just thought it was a politicized issue and they opposed making a formal statement. . . . Why do we have to do that? Why can't, you know, those people who are interested in it help the immigrants or refugees? They can do their own thing, but like you don't have to make it a church-wide thing. And so that was their perspective.[25]

25. Interview with a sanctuary participant on September 6, 2018.

Underlying this assumption is an interpretation that sanctuary practice should be an individual affair, not a corporate identity for the church. This does not imply that sanctuary is unimportant or invalid but that it is interpreted as voluntary actions, not political commitments. Behind this concern is a particular theology of the church and assumptions that frame the relationship between the church and the world, more specifically, the church and the public sphere. These assumptions, often implicit, reflect cultural beliefs about the relationship between religion and the state.

Church as a Body of Political-Ethical Practices

The ecclesial tensions, overt in this congregation and subtler in others, invite an analysis of the politics of the church itself. While most political theology focuses on why and how churches engage the realm of politics, William Cavanaugh represents a theological perspective that regards the church as a polity. Cavanaugh points to the early church's self-understanding as *ekklesia*—a public assembly, not a *collegium* or private club. He argues that the church conceived of itself as a distinctive public, an alternative to the Greek polis, inclusive of all the baptized, even those regarded as noncitizens (i.e., women and slaves). The early church was a political threat precisely because Christians regarded themselves not as a spiritualized, privatized community but as a public that represented the salvation of humanity.[26]

Cavanaugh traces the privatization of religion to the rise of the nation-state. Fueled by what Cavanaugh describes as the "myth of religious violence," the authority of the church was relegated to the spiritual realm, while the authority of the state was elevated over everything else. The social contract theory emerges as a way to protect the common good against religious extremism by appealing to human reason rather than religious doctrine to promote common interests. What this history ignores, Cavanaugh claims, is the way that the state

---

26. William Cavanaugh, "Church," in *The Blackwell Companion to Political Theology*, ed. Peter Scott and William Cavanaugh (Oxford: Blackwell, 2004), 369.

exercises power over bodies not through a unified conception of the good but through the threat of violence.[27]

In addition to the overt and oppressive ways the state exercises authority, Cavanaugh names subtle, performative, and systematic ways power functions in society. Following Michel Foucault, he argues that intermediary bodies such as churches, voluntary associations, and labor unions reinforce the power of state and capitalism through systemic discipline rather than overt domination.[28] Cavanaugh's suspicion of the state is important in the context of sanctuary. The need for sanctuary emerges from the failures of the state interwoven with failures of the economy to create conditions for inclusive human flourishing. The increased military presence at the border under President Trump represents an overt form of state-sanctioned violence to curb immigration. Abolitionist sanctuary movements noted earlier highlight more subtle ways the state exercises hegemonic power by pointing out how the privatization of prisons makes the detention of brown and black bodies profitable for those who hold economic and political power. Critics have pointed out how sanctuary churches themselves can unintentionally reinforce the criminalization of migrants by elevating an idealistic image of the "good migrant" worthy of protection (i.e., DACA recipients, hardworking parents) that does not include the full range of migrant experiences and identities.

So how does the church exercise resistance in this cultural milieu that easily and often invisibly co-opts it to reinforce a dominant neoliberal narrative? Like his mentor Stanley Hauerwas, Cavanaugh rejects the liberal expectation that churches translate their faith claims into publicly accessible discourse in order to engage in politics. He challenges foundational assumptions in modern Catholic social thought represented by John Courtney Murray for paradoxically reinforcing a church-state dualism in order to put forth an argument for the public role of the church. Murray maintains the separation of church and state

27. William Cavanaugh, "Religious Violence as Modern Myth," *Political Theology* 15 no. 6 (2014): 486–502.

28. William Cavanaugh, *Theo-political Imagination: Discovering the Liturgy as a Political Act in an Age of Global Consumerism* (London: T&T Clark, 2002).

by distinguishing society from the state and arguing that the church can and should influence politics through social engagement while also respecting the autonomy of the state.[29]

Unconvinced that the state is a reliable protector of the common good, Cavanaugh prefers the Augustinian formation of two cities. Augustine regards the state and church to be eschatologically provisional expressions of God's plan for salvation. Imagining the relationship of church and state temporally reinforces the unified history of salvation, which the church manifests imperfectly in time and space. Cavanaugh suggests, "Any adequate ecclesiology must acknowledge the political implications of two crucial theological data: first, there is no separate history of politics apart from the history of salvation; and second, the church is indispensable to the history of salvation."[30] Against this backdrop of salvation history, the church and state are not so much separate, static institutions but "rival performances," a tragedy of sin and a comedy of the world's redemption.[31]

Emphasizing performance, Cavanaugh develops an ecclesiology of embodied practices that manifest the drama of paschal mystery as a disruption to the state. In his early work, Cavanaugh presented the Eucharist as a political practice of resistance to violence. He focused on the church's role in resisting torture in the context of Chile under the dictatorship of Augusto Pinochet. Cavanaugh argues that the practice of the Eucharist created an alternative political experience. This political consciousness allowed the church to resist torture by publicly excommunicating members of Pinochet's regime and performing street liturgies that announced the church's opposition to violence. For Cavanaugh, the practice of the Eucharist not only cultivated virtues to carry into the public sphere but enacted its own politics of opposition.[32]

29. John Courtney Murray, *We Hold These Truths: Catholic Reflections on the American Proposition* (New York: Sheed and Ward, 1960).

30. Cavanaugh, "Church," 393.

31. William Cavanaugh, "From One City to Two: Christian Reimagining of Political Space," *Political Theology* 7, no. 3 (2006): 299–321, at 315.

32. William Cavanaugh, *Torture and Eucharist* (Oxford: Blackwell Publishing, 1998).

Stout, like Cavanaugh, challenges guiding narratives of the liberal tradition that perceive religious diversity to be a threat. He likewise rejects the assumption that the state is neutral and that tolerance toward pluralism is best expressed through translating one's commitments into reasonably accessible claims. However, Stout takes issue with Cavanaugh for failing to distinguish between secularism as an ideology and the historical process of secularization. Stout fears that antisecularism drives Christian theologians to set up a rigid boundary between the church and the public sphere.[33]

Offering a theological critique of Cavanagh's ecclesiology, Christopher Insole points out a limitation of conceiving the church as a set of virtuous practices, which Cavanaugh accepts from Hauerwas and MacIntyre, namely, that God's activity is located too squarely in the church itself, without allowing God's surprising action in the world and among strangers.[34] Enacting sanctuary alongside nonreligious activists and organizations, as well as other faith communities, has also transformed the church. Yukich names this well in her approach to sanctuary as a multi-targeted social movement. One of the ways congregations aimed to transform their public identity was to emphasize the interfaith dimension of sanctuary. While Cavanaugh's eschatology tempers any leanings toward Christian triumphalism, in his overemphasis on the particularity of the church, Cavanagh does not account for the interreligious aspect of sanctuary. Stout argues this point as well, grounded in his observation of how interfaith coalitions come together around civil rights and social justice.[35]

Criticisms notwithstanding, Cavanaugh is particularly helpful in naming the ways sanctuary is not only an exercise of the church's public voice, but sanctuary is a way of the church *being* political through its practices. Embracing Foucault's analysis of power allows him to highlight the ways neoliberalism permeates social movements like sanctuary, even through the theologies of progressive churches. Cavanaugh's ecclesiology also points to the centrality of practices as a way to communicate and

33. Stout, *Democracy and Tradition*, 114.
34. Christopher J. Insole, "Discerning the Theopolitical: A Response to Cavanaugh's Reimagining of Political Space," *Political Theology* 7, no. 3: (2006): 323–35, at 333.
35. Stout, *Blessed Are the Organized*.

reproduce the church's alternative vision of society. Consider the performative aspects of the sanctuary strategies highlighted so far. St. John the Evangelist not only declared sanctuary in written word, the church members performed an interfaith street liturgy, harnessing the particular rituals of Ash Wednesday to enact a political stance. The congregation who displayed the sanctuary banner next to Black Lives Matter and the rainbow flag did not rely on rational argumentation but a visible, evocative action to name their identity, theological and political.

Another unmistakable aspect of the St. John's declaration is the use of storytelling. It was a story of St. John the Evangelist—a progressive church in the Mission District for whom the value of inclusivity means creating a space for immigrants, the LGBTQ community, and unhoused people. It was a story about Christianity, a community naming their need for repentance as they enter into the sacred period of Lent. Significantly, this story was ritualized by an interfaith group, amplifying its significance beyond the Christian community. The story was not only religious. The march and declaration also spoke to a national narrative. This is a nation of immigrants, a champion for human rights. Connecting the Christian narrative of welcoming the stranger and loving one's neighbor to the national narrative issues an ethical mandate with public significance. Declaring sanctuary calls the nation to be a refuge for migrants, to be on the side of human rights, regardless of nationality. Finally, the sanctuary march and declaration were themselves performances of religious belief in a public space, demonstrating a different way of being religious and a different way of being political, one that invites diverse communities to engage in the conversation on what it means to be a sanctuary city.

"It's in Our DNA"—Sanctuary and Ecclesial Identity

But I just want to say that the sanctuary stuff for us was already in motion well before Trump. So it's much more systemic for us, and it's not just about the resistance and responding to Trump. It's much deeper. It goes much deeper than that, as part of a sense, our growing sense, that it's always been there, but it's just gotten more profound. . . . [Referring to their hospitality to unhoused people in the community] so many of the folks who come in and, and are part of that community are also immigrants, not only, I mean it's a real mix, the sense of who we are, who we identify as, who is the church and, and it's not us in the neighborhood. It's like we are the neighborhood, and the neighborhood increasingly is us. We've always been gay-friendly and being gay is part of our DNA, but now being the neighborhood is also part of our DNA. The whole practice of sanctuary; it's in our DNA.[36]

Some churches experienced the declaration of sanctuary as an obvious expression of their identity. Sanctuary was part of their story, connected to the sanctuary story of San Francisco and interwoven with their faith narratives. These congregations had already been taking pro-immigrant stances through advocacy and accompaniment. A small number of individuals had participated in the earlier sanctuary movement in the 1980s, which informed their identity as a church. The majority of people I interviewed still named the election of Donald Trump as the impetus for declaring sanctuary. However, for these churches, it provided not so much an interruption of identity but a rereading of their story.

One sanctuary leader who saw sanctuary as an expression of his congregation's radical inclusivity told me about the church's role in supporting gay men during the 1980s AIDS crisis in San Francisco. Ostracized by society, many of them rejected by their own families, these men found refuge in the church, which became a place of welcome, safety, and support. The church did not describe this practice as sanctuary at the time; however, the declaration of sanctuary prompted them to reread their history and conclude that they had always been a sanctuary. Another pastor described this experience within his congregation and added that "LGBTQ people in San Francisco are immigrants. They come here for acceptance and in many cases, physical safety.[37]

---

36. Interview with a sanctuary participant on September 30, 2018.
37. Interview with a sanctuary participant on August 5, 2019.

A number of progressive churches named themselves as sanctuary to the LGBTQ community, expressed not only through their history of inclusion but also through their advocacy for their rights. This stance is multidirectional. They are not only providing sanctuary from a hostile society but also see themselves as a refuge for people who have been marginalized or harmed by religion. One pastor described a practice of holding space for people who do not feel welcomed in the church. He had developed a practice of accompaniment beyond the church walls, going to people and offering prayer or just listening. In doing so, he sees himself as bringing church to people who did not experience themselves as welcome in a religious space. In this context, sanctuary not only provided a hermeneutic for rereading the congregation's history, but it also informed their political and ecclesial identity, giving direction in the present and future.

Narratives not only shape identity but also have the power to shape moral action and political consciousness, as Maria Pia Lara demonstrates in her focus on feminist narratives. She points out that feminists, excluded from the dominant public sphere, used biography as a political tool, enlarging what counts as public concern.[38] Paul Ricoeur has argued that narratives anchor our subjectivity in time, connecting memory with a sense of purpose for the future. Further, he argues that memory is an interpretive exercise and new interpretations render different ways of imagining the future.[39] So as these churches interpret their history through the lens of a sanctuary commitment, they reinforce their identity and gain a sense of purpose for the future.

Church as a Bearer of Memory

Political theologian Johann Baptist Metz distinguishes between the church who remembers and the church who forgets. Writing in Germany after World War II, he is particularly concerned with liberal theologies that allow the church to forget Auschwitz. This church fails to face the question of theodicy—where is God in suffering?—because it

---

38. Pia Lara, *Moral Textures.*

39. Paul Ricoeur, *Time and Narrative*, trans. Kathleen Blamey and David Pellauer, 3 vols. (Chicago: University of Chicago Press, 1984–1988).

has lost touch with its central narrative. Jesus's suffering, death, and resurrection at the heart of the Christian story is a "dangerous memory." It is dangerous, Metz argues, because it is interruptive, pointing to an alternative history where the oppressed have reason to hope. The church who forgets loses its sociopolitical vocation to announce a liberating hope in solidarity with those who suffer.

In order for the church to retrieve its critical function, it must embrace its Jewish roots, particularly the prophetic role of memory or "anamnestic reason." The church's preference for the instrumentalist, disembodied reason of the Enlightenment is rooted in its early adoption of a Hellenistic worldview. Anamnestic reason, by contrast, is situated in the particular narrative and tradition of a community, encouraging reflexivity and accountability to the past. As a bearer of the dangerous memory of Christ's death and resurrection, Christianity announces the liberation of the oppressed—not in a utopian future but concretely in history. This hope is subversive, unlike the hope promoted by modernity, which places its faith in future progress and human achievement. Metz argues:

> The Church must understand and justify itself as the public witness and bearer of the tradition of a dangerous memory of freedom in the "systems" of our emancipative society. . . . Memory [is]. . . the fundamental form of expression of Christian faith. . . . It is not a middle-class counter-figure to hope. On the contrary, it anticipates the future as a future of those who are oppressed, without hope and doomed to fail.[40]

Metz is critical of the Enlightenment's emphasis on instrumental reason and future-oriented progress that reads history from the perspective of winners. However, he embraces the overall project of the Enlightenment, including secularization, because he regards this as an aspect of the church's own liberation. This context allows the church to open itself to the world, to nontheological sources of knowledge,

---

40. Johann Baptist Metz, *Faith in History and Society: Toward a Fundamental Practical Theology* (New York: Seabury, 1980), 90.

and in a critical engagement with the world, the church can become what it is meant to become—an institution of sociopolitical freedom.[41] Grounded in this view, Metz argues for a transformation of the church, away from its overly hierarchical structure that encourages laity to be passive consumers of religion rather than subjects in the church. This passivity, coupled with a privatization of faith, marks what Metz describes as bourgeois religion. Modeling the opposite of the bourgeois church that has lost its prophetic dimension, Metz lifts up the base communities of Latin America.[42]

Metz's positive yet critical view of modernity makes his political theology in some ways more helpful than Cavanaugh's. Metz addresses the context of pluralism with humility, "in the pluralistic society, it cannot be the socio-critical attitude of the Church to proclaim one positive societal order as an absolute norm. It can consist only in effecting within this society a critical, liberating freedom."[43] At the same time, Cavanaugh's emphasis on embodiment counters a forgetfulness of space, which I consider to be as problematic as the church's forgetfulness of time, Metz's primary concern. Charles Pinches regards Cavanaugh and his Hauerwasian colleagues as overcoming an insidious Gnosticism, characterized by a rejection of the physical world in favor of the transcendent—a view that persists in Christian theology.[44] This concern sets up the focus of the next chapter, which argues for embodied solidarity rooted in story-sharing.

Metz is particularly helpful in understanding the role of memory and narrative in the congregations who embraced sanctuary as a hermeneutic to reread their own history. The shift toward narrative provides an alternative entry into public discourse beyond rational argumentation and translation. Metz's sociopolitical ecclesiology overcomes

41. Johann Baptist Metz, "Religion and Society in the Light of a Political Theology," *Harvard Theological Review* 61, no. 4 (1968): 507–23.

42. Johann Baptist Metz, *The Emergent Church: The Future of Christianity in a Postbourgeois World*, trans. Peter Mann (New York: Crossroad, 1981).

43. Metz, "Religion and Society," 521.

44. Charles Robert Pinches, "Hauerwas and Political Theology: The Next Generation," *Journal of Religious Ethics* 36, no. 3 (2008): 511–42.

some of the limitations of the liberal tradition but encourages social engagement in a way that speaks to a secular and interreligious context. Metz explains, "The 'mediation' of the memory of suffering is always practical. It is never purely argumentative, but always narrative, in form, in other words, it takes the form of dangerous and liberating stories."[45]

Mary Doak elaborates on how narrative functions in public theology, drawing on Metz, Hauerwas, and Robert Thiemann. Without glossing over difference, Doak notes the ways these thinkers reinforce the idea that "Christian narratives take precedence in forming our beliefs and values, but those beliefs and values must also be related to the specific historical contexts for which they provide meaning and direction."[46] She takes this hermeneutical principle to mean that Christian narratives and national narratives require a mutual coherence in order to be subjected to mutual critique. Doak's double-narrative approach insists on a narrative public theology that interprets national narratives as a "story within a story" of God's action in history. She carefully rejects the idea that there is a single national narrative and claims a positive role of Christian narratives in the public debate around the nation's values, goals, and identity. Doak offers concrete examples of theologians who have articulated a narrative public theology based on the following criteria:

> In addition to being (1) publicly accessible and criticizable, it should (2) engage the issues of public life with the resources of a particular religious tradition (here primarily in the form of a narrative of God's purposes in history). In thus relating public life to the divine purposes for history, this theology would ensure that (3) the religious perspective enables evaluation and critique of the nation's purposes and actions, while (4) allowing the demands of public life to provide a further specification of the meaning of the religious narrative.[47]

45. Metz, *Faith in History and Society*, 110.
46. Mary Doak, *Reclaiming Narrative for Public Theology* (Albany, NY: State University of New York Press, 2004), 164.
47. Doak, *Reclaiming Narrative*, 175.

Doak's insights are helpful for understanding the role of narrative in the sanctuary movement and the potential of narrative for public impact. The sanctuary movement, in many ways, offers a story within a story. It interprets the national narrative as one that not only embraces immigrants but sees them as protagonists in the story. It challenges the United States to live up to its commitments to human rights, freedom, and equal opportunity. This story is situated in the larger Christian narrative of welcoming the stranger, encountering God in the marginalized, and becoming a community that transcends nationality.

Doak's emphasis on national narratives is both helpful in the context of sanctuary and also limited in its ability to speak to the international context that situates this movement. If we assume that the sanctuary movement has created an alternative public space where the interests of two communities—North American churches along with migrants and asylum seekers—are intertwined, then this context provides an additional dialogue partner. How might the narratives of migrants interwoven with the narratives of nation and church inform the sanctuary movement?

When comparing the sanctuary movement in the 1980s and the New Sanctuary Movement, the shifts in strategy are notable. However, the central role of migrant testimony has been consistent. One might argue that the sanctuary movement was built on the willingness of migrants to share their stories of suffering and struggle. Coutin describes the role of migrant testimony in fostering a conversion experience among sanctuary congregations who, informed by liberation theology, saw the poor and vulnerable as closer to God than themselves.[48]

Yukich similarly observes the role of storytelling in the New Sanctuary Movement as a means for promoting religious conversion, generating empathy and involvement.[49] She argues that this strategy is only successful if storytelling becomes *story-sharing*.[50] Story-sharing involves ongoing interpersonal contact and the formation of relationships, which goes beyond listening to an individual's story. Many churches embrace this in their commitment to accompaniment, making the

48. Coutin, *Culture of Protest*, 71.
49. Yukich, *One Family under God*, 86.
50. Yukich, *One Family under God*, 86.

encounter with the migrant the starting point of a relationship marked by walking with them. She uses sociological theory to argue that interpersonal contact can have a strong impact on people's perceptions of other groups. But she argues, "However, casual contact—such as hearing an immigrant tell his story at one's church—may have neutral or even negative effects on attitudes about the other. It is the sharing of experiences that comes through more prolonged, intimate contact that has greater potential to make people's attitudes more inclusive."[51]

A number of people I talked to identified the importance of encounter in shaping their commitment to sanctuary. Some described the experience of hearing a "migrant in the pulpit" as a moment that galvanized their commitment or generated empathy among the congregation. However, I observed a widespread challenge of getting more congregants involved with accompaniment. Usually, a handful of sanctuary leaders did the actual work of sanctuary accompaniment—showing up at immigration hearings and providing transportation, meals, and childcare for sponsored families. This raises a question, in light of Yukich's point, about the use of migrant testimony as a strategy. What relationship is formed with the "other"—in this case, the migrant in the pulpit—when people hear their story but do not participate in the story-sharing? If sanctuary churches are to create a compelling public theology, the narratives of faith and nation must reconcile themselves with the narratives of those seeking sanctuary. This cannot be accomplished through a single encounter but rather calls forth a deeper solidarity rooted in embodied relationships.[52]

An Ecclesiology of Prophetic Witness

Pope Francis's field hospital ecclesiology connects prophetic witness to closeness with the poor formed by ongoing encounter with those on the margins. Bringing his ecclesiology into conversation with Metz,

---

51. Yukich, *One Family under God,* 87.

52. The next chapter will take up these questions in more depth, offering a critical analysis of sanctuary practices and the ecclesial contexts in which they occur.

Cavanaugh, and the operant theologies in sanctuary practice presents a publicly engaged church that evangelizes through attractive witness and that is also continually evangelized by those on the margins of society but at the center of the Gospel. Francis is critical of the liberal privatization of religion and defends Christian humanism as a resource for secular culture.[53] But unlike his predecessor, Benedict XVI, Francis does not emphasize reason as the primary way faith should impact the public sphere.[54] Rather, Francis, like Cavanaugh, emphasizes attractive witness that comes from and is constantly renewed by encounter with Christ in and through those who are poor.

Francis rejects a church that retreats from engaging the world, whose members have become apathetic, forgetting the missionary impulse that springs from the Gospel. Stressing the evangelizing role of each Christian and distinguishing it from "proselytism," Francis's field hospital church shares the Gospel by "attraction."[55] He defends the social dimension of religion, arguing that authentic faith concerns the integral development of all people and the building of a just society.[56] At the same time, he rejects a worldly church, one that is mostly concerned with money and prestige, with preserving itself as an institution rather than serving the people of God.[57] Here Francis echoes Metz and Cavanaugh, who, in different ways, articulate a postbourgeois ecclesiology that resists consumerism and individualism through countercultural witness.

Like Metz, Francis connects the church's prophetic dimension to the memory of Jesus's life, death, and resurrection. Stressing the centrality of memory and faith, Francis describes, "The believer is essentially 'one who remembers.' "[58] Celebrating the Eucharist and staying rooted in the Gospel provide ongoing renewal of faith through memory. Although

---

53. EG, 68.

54. Jürgen Habermas and Joseph Ratzinger (Pope Benedict XVI), *The Dialectics of Secularization: On Reason and Religion*, trans. Brian McNeil (San Francisco: Ignatius Press, 2006).

55. EG, 14.

56. EG, 183.

57. EG, 95.

58. EG, 13.

Francis often repeats a guiding epistemological principle, "time is greater than space," his attention to the material reality of exclusion and his commitment to physical proximity infuses his ecclesiology with spatial metaphors. Guided by a dialectical vision, Francis recognizes time and space as inseparable. However, Francis's association of time with process and space with the consolidation of power does not account for the subtle way that sanctuary practices construct alternative public spaces to disrupt power. Francis's field hospital ecclesiology is rooted in a preferential option for the poor; however, it privileges the voices of sanctuary seekers, providing a basis for solidarity out of which sanctuary is constructed.

Francis regards the poor as the evangelizers of the church.[59] For Francis, the category of "the poor"[60] refers to those who have been marginalized by unjust social structures and therefore can be appropriately applied to migrants and refugees who experience not only economic exclusion but political and cultural exclusion. A preferential option for the poor, for Francis, involves a rejection of an economy that kills and the construction of a culture of encounter. As he observes: "Only on the basis of this real and sincere closeness can we properly accompany the poor on their path of liberation. Only this will ensure that 'in every Christian community the poor feel at home. Would not this approach be the greatest and most effective presentation of the good news of the kingdom?' "[61]

This statement captures the meaning of sanctuary as prophetic witness. When the church becomes a community where the poor feel at home, it gives witness to the kingdom. For Francis, this is achieved through closeness to those who are marginalized, making the distinction between storytelling and story-sharing critical in considering the practice of migrant testimony. Solidarity cannot be achieved through observation or "sporadic acts of generosity";[62] for Francis, "It means

---

59. EG, 198.

60. The next chapter will engage in critical debates about referring to "the poor" as a broad, abstract category.

61. EG, 199.

62. FT, 116.

thinking and acting in terms of community."[63] Solidarity must be embodied in concrete relationships. For Pope Francis, the ability of the church to witness to the joy of the Gospel is something constantly renewed through relationship with those on the margins. But the true evangelizers of the Gospel are those seeking sanctuary—the economic or political refugee, the unhoused person, the outcast.

63. FT, 116.

Chapter 3

Sanctuary as Embodied Solidarity

n the spring of 2019, I joined three women at a coffee shop to plan
a three-part reflection series on sanctuary. The series was designed
to promote awareness and expand engagement among members of
two neighboring sanctuary churches. Two women were staff members
of one of the churches, and the other woman, like me, was a volunteer
involved in accompaniment and advocacy. All of us United States
citizens and with relative economic privilege, our identities reflect the
majority of people I interviewed for this project. This morning we were
meeting with an organizer from Faith in Action to plan the second of
three sessions on faith-based community organizing as it relates to the
churches' sanctuary commitment.

"Power is about interweaving stories," the community organizer
explained to us. It is rooted in a "one-on-one" or sacred conversation,
which builds relational power by getting people to talk about what
is important to them and discovering common interests. Reflecting
on the task of helping us organize joint sanctuary activities together
with another mostly white, upper-middle-class church, the organizer
continued, "The challenge here is that organizing is most effective
when it motivates people to identify shared self-interest. It begins when
people who are most impacted by the issue identify what matters to

them and builds relational power from there." Our conversation shifted toward the topic of power. How do we generate a conversation in our churches about race, class, gender, and citizenship status and how these realities impact our sanctuary commitment? A member of the church staff suggested that members of the congregation might shy away from difficult conversations on white privilege and class power, but we all agreed that these conversations were necessary for fostering solidarity.

At the coffee shop, we reflected on the first of three sessions on community organizing, which, a week prior, had brought together a dozen people from two sanctuary churches. During introductions at that first meeting, the facilitator asked us to share why we came to the session. Most people spoke about injustices toward immigrants—the separation of families, the terror of being deported, the condition of detention centers near the border—and the sense of obligation, as people of faith or as citizens, to do something. One person shared their own immigration story. One couple was new to the church and wanted to meet people and understand what sanctuary is about.

Our planning meeting at the coffee shop, where we discussed the topic of power, prompted a shift in the conversation at the second meeting held later that week. Instead of asking about sanctuary explicitly, the two facilitators encouraged the participants to reflect on a time we needed mercy. The conversation shifted toward our own experiences of vulnerability, varied as they were—the end of a relationship, loss of a job, feeling like an outsider. This interweaving of such stories revealed a fundamental human interdependence that is the basis of solidarity as defined by Catholic social teaching.

In my interviews with sanctuary leaders, Catholic and Protestant, solidarity emerged as a recurring theme, evoked explicitly and implicitly when describing the meaning and purpose of sanctuary. Despite this espoused theology,[1] there are barriers to actualizing solidarity

---

1. In this chapter, I draw upon the distinction between espoused and operant theology made in Helen Cameron, Deborah Bhatti, Catherine Duce, James Sweeney, and Clare Watkins, *Talking about God in Practice: Theological Action Research and Practical Theology* (London: SCM Press, 2010). The authors name four voices of theology: formal, normative, espoused, and operant. Cameron et. al., *Theological Action Research*, 54.

through sanctuary. The sanctuary movement has exposed unexamined assumptions around representation, participation, and power in Christian theology and practice. Faith-based sanctuary, past and present, has been critiqued as paternalistic, reinforcing the "otherness" of migrants under the banner of solidarity with the poor.[2] Critics, including those who identify with sanctuary, have pointed to the reality that the sanctuary movement of the 1980s and today has been largely led by largely white congregations with economic and political power.

Reflecting on the period of sanctuary in the 1980s, Susan Bibler Coutin reported that participants themselves had critiqued paternalism in the movement as counter to their commitment to solidarity with Central Americans. In her critical analysis of the theology behind sanctuary, Coutin suggests: "Although solidarity opposed imperialism, isolationism, charitable approaches, and exploitation, it contained a mystification."[3] Informed by an interpretation of liberation theology that regarded the poor and oppressed as "closer to God,"[4] Central American migrants provided an impetus for sanctuary activists to deepen their own faith. Yet reinforcing the migrants' otherness obscures interdependence as the basis for solidarity. The mystification to which Coutin refers was reinforced through refugees publicly telling their story, a practice that has been interpreted in a variety of ways,

---

2. I will elaborate on some of these critiques in the chapter, but I wanted to clarify how I am using the term paternalism as a barrier to solidarity. Paternalistic approaches to sanctuary consciously or unconsciously maintain or reinforce an imbalance of power between those providing sanctuary and those receiving it. Susan Bibler Coutin and Robin Lorentzen both describe critiques among sanctuary activists of charitable approaches to sanctuary, which these activists associate with paternalism. See Susan Bibler Coutin, *The Culture of Protest: Religious Activism and the U.S. Sanctuary Movement* (Boulder: Westview Press, 1993); and Robin Lorentzen, *Women in the Sanctuary Movement* (Philadelphia: Temple University Press, 1991). Hector Perla refers to paternalistic aspects of the sanctuary movement that disregarded the agency of Central Americans, which he regards as central to the success of sanctuary as a transnational movement. See Héctor Perla, Jr. "Si Nicaragua Venció, El Salvador Vencerá: Central American Agency in the Creation of the U.S.–Central American Peace and Solidarity Movement," *Latin American Research Review* 43, no. 2 (2008): 136–58, at 154.

3. Coutin, *Culture of Protest,* 186.

4. Coutin, *Culture of Protest,* 187.

from empowering to exploitative.[5] The dynamics of solidarity versus paternalism are reflected not only in how the church manifests itself in sanctuary practice but are embedded within operant ecclesiologies that persist in the current sanctuary movement. So how do we build solidarity among mostly white, economically resourced congregations? What kinds of practices build this solidarity? What ecclesiology reinforces this solidarity?

This chapter will highlight some tensions around inclusion and representation in the practice of sanctuary—who decides, who speaks for the group, whose experiences are privileged in the discernment. While theologies of sanctuary embrace solidarity as a central principle, one can observe barriers to solidarity in sanctuary practice. Critics within and external to the sanctuary movement have observed and denounced paternalistic practices that expose migrants to risk or obscure their agency. I will examine the interplay between belief and practice in this context before examining barriers to solidarity that are mirrored in power dynamics within ecclesial structures. Drawing upon a feminist ethic of risk, I will analyze concrete examples of sanctuary declaration and practice and point toward an ecclesiology of embodied solidarity.

Who Decides? Who Speaks? Who Does the Work? Church, Power, and Sanctuary Practices

Mary[6] and I sat at a large table surrounded by books on social justice and spirituality. The space, adjacent to the church, is typically used for spiritual direction, prayer groups, book discussions, and events. Just a few weeks prior to our conversation, the space was a temporary home to an asylum-seeking family from Mexico. Mary, a lay woman, began a pastoral staff position in the church shortly after the congregation had

---

5. I will explore both arguments in the chapter. For a critical analysis of migrant testimony, see Serin Houston and Charlotte Morse, "The Ordinary and Extraordinary: Producing Migrant Inclusion and Exclusion in US Sanctuary Movements," *Studies in Social Justice* 11, no. 1 (2017): 27–47.

6. Name changed for anonymity.

decided to house the family as an expression of their public sanctuary commitment. I asked her to describe what it was like to step into this work, and she replied, "When I started my work, I remember going into the [center] and it dawned on me the gravity of our commitment. I could see [the center] was chaotic. It was a mess. It was definitely lived in by a family with multiple kids, including a toddler."[7]

Mary's predecessor, Anne,[8] also a lay woman, had been the person leading the church's sanctuary efforts, which relied on a small number of lay volunteers who met regularly to discuss opportunities for advocacy and accompaniment. This group provided direct assistance to the sanctuary family—driving them to appointments, cooking meals, and searching for more stable housing. Despite her inability to speak Spanish, Anne was the point of contact for the sanctuary family.

Mary, a former educator, had lived for a short time in Central America. This experience helped her establish a relationship with the sanctuary family because not only did it afford her the ability to communicate in Spanish, but it also allowed her to connect to the experience of being on a journey and needing companionship. Mary remembered her time in Central America marked by profound experiences of hospitality as the basis for her sanctuary commitment.

> I just think of the incredible privilege I've had being welcomed into people's lives and stories and homes time and time again. When I was in college, I, after some deliberation, decided to study abroad and it completely reoriented me as a person. In terms of my faith expanding, everything. But that was largely due to the encounter that I had with people who really humbly opened their doors . . . [and] so gently instructed me in their histories and political dynamics and the struggle to survive. And it showed completely their dignity and the violence of injustice and certain ways that our country or government or my lifestyle or whatever, we were all kind of interwoven and complicit. I felt this incredible connection with these people who generously

---

7. Interview with sanctuary participant, August 10, 2018.
8. Name changed for anonymity.

were vulnerable and sharing not only their pride and their joy, their families and their work, but also these things that maybe I wouldn't have shared so easily with other people, wounds and trauma, history like that.[9]

Mary experienced radical hospitality—not only through people welcoming her into their homes but also through their vulnerability, trust, and openness. Mary went on to describe how she developed a relationship with the sanctuary family in San Francisco and how this gradually revealed the meaning of sanctuary as an experience of kinship.

It all came kind of haphazardly you know. It's just learning along the way. . . . Now there's a sense of kinship and sharing. And I think being in a city that is high powered, that is accomplishment-based, that is driven by progress and efficiency . . . that's wealthy. I don't totally feel at home here either, you know, coming from this line of work, the way of life that I came from. I feel actually more at home with [the mother] and her kids.[10]

Mary's articulation of kinship was echoed by others who connected their story with the story of those seeking sanctuary. A number of people I interviewed talked about their personal or family immigration story as the basis for solidarity. Others discussed an experience of marginalization due to race, ethnicity, or sexuality in their connection to sanctuary. A frequent challenge I observed across denominations was expanding a personal experience of solidarity to an institutional commitment. In Mary's congregation, like several others, the sanctuary efforts were led by less than a dozen volunteers. In addition to the issue of participation, Mary's experience points to the issue of representation and authority. Specifically, the people doing the hands-on work of sanctuary are not necessarily the decision-makers or public faces of the commitment. In Mary's case, the official representative of the

---

9. Interview with sanctuary participant, August 10, 2018.
10. Interview with sanctuary participant, August 10, 2018.

congregation, including its sanctuary declaration, was the ordained pastor. The pastor was supportive of the church's sanctuary commitment and expressed the desire for more widespread engagement among parishioners.

When I spoke to the pastor about the process of declaring sanctuary, he insisted that the process was initiated by Anne, Mary's predecessor, whose passion for sanctuary was ignited by the election of Donald Trump. She brought the issue to the parish staff, who decided to declare sanctuary on behalf of the church. While he felt strongly that the declaration of sanctuary flowed from the identity of the congregation as a "progressive Vatican II parish," the pastor expressed regret over not involving the community in the discernment and process of declaring sanctuary. "The impetus [for sanctuary] came from the staff and not so much from the people. . . . If you could create something where impetus comes from the people you know, that'd be much better. And then the staff is part of it."[11]

He went on to describe his vision of church leadership, informed by the ecclesiology of Vatican II that empowers the laity to participate actively in the decision-making and life of the church. He talked about the changing role of the pastor, from one with absolute authority to one of service and shared power. He even suggested that it would be good for the church to have a college of laity along with the college of cardinals who could take part in the governance of the church at the highest levels.

The example above highlights complexity around who decides and who represents the public aspect of sanctuary and who does the work to support that commitment. Despite this congregation's explicit commitment to gender equality along with a progressive theology of the laity, both pastor and lay staff member point to the disproportionate distribution of labor involved in the work of sanctuary. From the pastor's perspective, the lay woman decided to declare sanctuary, an action that both affirmed their commitment to lay leadership but failed to reflect the church's commitment to broaden participation among the faithful.

---

11. Interview with sanctuary participant, October 15, 2018.

The pastor is the spokesperson for the congregation's identity—he signs the declaration as the official public voice of the congregation—but a laywoman, with the support of a few volunteers, delivers the meals, helps with childcare, and addresses the daily messiness that sanctuary entails.

Other scholars have paid attention to the role of gender in the sanctuary movement, though not from an ecclesiological perspective. In her analysis of gender roles in the sanctuary movement of the 1980s, Coutin observed that men were frequently positioned as the spokespersons for the movement, while women did much of the work. This, she argues, expressed and reinforced an implicit assumption that men are more suited for public engagement while women occupy the domestic sphere. Sanctuary workers themselves point out that women take up the work of nurturing and caregiving because this fits into the roles they've been socialized to adopt.[12]

Writing on sanctuary in the 1980s, Robin Lorentzen describes it as primarily a women-led social movement. However, she demonstrates how women's leadership and contribution was frequently obscured in favor of male representation. Writing on the sanctuary movement in Chicago, she compares the Tucson approach of direct humanitarian assistance to Chicago's emphasis on widespread political change. Women assume humanitarian and political caretaking roles, providing direct care to refugees as well as organizing and networking. Especially in the case of Tucson, where John Fife and Jim Corbett were seen by many as the originators and leaders of the movement, Lorentzen observes dissatisfaction among some women for the public emphasis on men that obscured their contribution.[13]

Lorentzen suggests that women's approach to leadership, characterized by intentional power-sharing and democratic processes, contributed to differences among women-led and male-led or mixed-gender sanctuary sites. She points specifically to the Chicago sites led by women religious as modeling a partnership approach that was overtly critical of paternalistic approaches to sanctuary that failed to recognize the agency of refugees and wider political aims of the

---

12. Coutin, *Culture of Protest*, 167.
13. Lorentzen, *Women in the Sanctuary Movement*, chapter 3.

movement. She also noted that women religious consistently saw the connection between feminism and sanctuary, both aimed at liberation of oppressed people. This emphasis on feminism caused friction on at least one occasion between women refugees and feminist sanctuary leaders, who did not share the aims of feminism as defined by white, middle-class women.[14]

Among the twelve congregations represented in the project, there are diverse ecclesial expressions of leadership and gender—in terms of official church structure reinforced by both formal theology and local practice. I had anticipated that the hierarchically structured churches would have followed a top-down approach to declaring sanctuary, while the more congregationally structured churches would follow a bottom-up approach. Although a number of congregational churches did approach the sanctuary decision by way of a vote, others did not. And while the hierarchical structure of churches mattered in terms of sanctuary declaration and practice, the aforementioned example reveals the complexity around how sanctuary was decided.

For example, one church went through a lengthy process of lay-led discernment, yet, when I asked the lay leader how they decided to declare sanctuary, she replied without reservation, "The pastor decided, of course." Some congregations had the support of a larger governing body, while others did not. For example, the Episcopal diocese of California had declared sanctuary broadly, inviting local churches to discern how to apply the commitment to their context. The Evangelical Lutheran Church of America had moved from a commitment described as AMMPARO (Accompany Migrant Minors with Protection, Advocacy, Representation, and Opportunities) to an official declaration of sanctuary during the time frame of this study.[15] Yet, episcopal or denominational support did not override or determine the process by which a congregation declared sanctuary. I observed congregations within these denominations who, at the time of the study, had not embraced sanctuary.

---

14. Lorentzen, *Women in the Sanctuary Movement*, chapter 6.

15. The ELCA declared itself a sanctuary body on August 7, 2019, being the first North American denomination to declare sanctuary on that level.

Representation and Power in the Church

The complexity revealed in how these congregations decide, declare, and practice sanctuary invites an analysis of power. In this section, I focus on Catholic ecclesiology and theologies of gender to analyze how power dynamics in the church impact the way the church expresses and practices sanctuary. Pope Francis's field hospital ecclesiology calls for practices of embodied solidarity; yet Francis's dialectical conception of gender reinforces a hierarchical ecclesiology that can separate the concrete work of sanctuary from those who speak for the church. I will explore why the dynamics of power and production matter in sanctuary practice before critically examining Catholic theologies of gender and church. Later in this chapter, I argue that the material work of sanctuary must inform the theological reflection and identity of the sanctuary congregation in order to ground the institutional commitment in concrete practices of solidarity.

In her research on how Catholics experience power dynamics in the church, Angela Coco analyzes the culturally constructed relationship between gender, work, and power in an ecclesial context.[16] Women, she argues, are socialized to take on the work of production, either physically through motherhood or symbolically through nurturing and service. Within a capitalist, patriarchal system, women's labor, often invisible and undervalued, frees men to assume positions of authority and public influence.[17] In an ecclesial context, the work of production revolves around material realities—from cleaning the church to balancing the budget—tasks which are devalued in comparison to the spiritual leadership of the ordained priest.[18]

In the particular context of sanctuary highlighted in this chapter, a lay woman does essential and messy work of production—making meals, cleaning up, coordinating volunteers and addressing the material

---

16. Angela Coco, *Catholics, Conflicts and Choices: An Exploration of Power Relations in the Catholic Church* (London: Routledge, 2013). Coco draws upon Marxist feminist theory in her analysis, particularly the thought of Maria Mies, "Social Origins of the Sexual Division of Labour," in *Women: The Last Colony*, ed. Maria Mies, Veronika Bennholdt-Thomsen, and Claudia von Werlhof (London: Zed Books, 1988), 65–95.

17. Coco, *Catholics, Conflicts and Choices*, 67.

18. Coco, *Catholics, Conflicts and Choices*, 67.

needs of the family but she does not speak as the official public voice of the church. The formal theology of this tradition excludes women from ordained ministry, instituting parameters around her ministerial leadership in the church. At the same time, the ecclesiology of Vatican II, evoked by the pastor in his reflection on the ideal process of declaring and practicing sanctuary, rejects a sharp division of material and spiritual labor in the church.

Lumen Gentium, the Second Vatican Council's Dogmatic Constitution on the Church, presents the church first as the people of God before distinguishing roles. The document further grounds all ministries, lay and ordained, as flowing from one's incorporation into the Body of Christ at baptism. Yet, as the example above demonstrates, embracing the formal teaching of Vatican II does not override the concrete experiences of power in the church, which are impacted by gender and other intersecting identities. Offering a feminist explanation for this contradiction, Natalie Watson claims:

> The ambiguous body symbolism used by the authors of *Lumen Gentium* is a profound source of alienation for women. The Church is defined as the body of Christ which is united by Christ as its head and under that condition celebrates the diversity of its members. For the church, traditionally often portrayed as female, to be defined as a body it has to be the body of Christ, a male body which, in addition to its denial of female bodiliness, is entirely dependent on its head, Christ.[19]

The gendered imagery of the church as mother and bride of Christ, which has biblical roots, became more pronounced in modern theological discourse under John Paul II.[20] Within John Paul II's theology

19. Natalie Watson, "A Feminist Critical Reading of the Ecclesiology of 'Lumen Gentium,'" in *Is There a Future for Feminist Theology?*, ed. Deborah F. Sawyer and Diane M. Collier, Studies in Theology and Sexuality 4 (Sheffield: Sheffield Academic Press, 1999), 79.

20. Tina Beattie interprets this shift within a broader debate on the significance of Vatican II. Joseph Ratzinger/Pope Benedict XVI and Hans Urs Von Balthasar emphasize continuity with tradition while reformist thinkers Karl Rahner and Yves

of the body, women and men are assumed to have universal, innate, and complementary characteristics that flow from their embodiment as female and male. This view, reinforced by Sacred Congregation for the Doctrine of Faith, rejects the distinction between biological sex and gender, as historically situated and culturally constructed.[21] Beyond theological anthropology, this understanding of gender influences Catholic ecclesiology in theoretical and practical ways.

Pope Francis has embraced maternal imagery for the church, pointing to Mary as a model of the church's open, nurturing, loving presence among all cultures.[22] Evangelization, he argues, should reflect the maternal quality of the church. Just as a mother listens to her children and speaks in a language they can understand, preachers should be attentive to culture and enter into a close relationship with recipients of their message.[23] Tina Beattie points out the paradox of asking male preachers to reflect the maternal face of the church while excluding women from formal leadership. Women remain in a symbolic role, perpetuating the elevated feminine characteristics of the church associated with motherhood, regardless of whether or not they are mothers. This ecclesiology is not only exclusionary of women but alienating:

> The elision of any significant distinction between womanhood and motherhood means that women remain trapped in the function of the womb—the role of providing space for others, while never occupying their own time and space in the human story. In other words, defined within this symbolic of the maternal, women do not change and develop through time; we do not incarnate the revelation of God in our particular cultures and

Congar offered a more progressive theology. Beattie argues that romanticized nuptial ecclesiology was a push back on reformist theology and feminism. See Tina Beattie, *New Catholic Feminism: Theology and Theory* (London: Routledge, 2006).

21. Sacred Congregation for the Doctrine of the Faith, "On the Collaboration of Men and Women," (May 31, 2004), at http://www.vatican.va.

22. EG, 284.

23. EG, 139–40.

contexts, but remain always available as the repository of men's fantasies of maternal nurture and feminine genius.[24]

Although Pope Francis has demonstrated interest in reforming church structures to create opportunities for women's voices in decision-making, his theology has not departed significantly from that of John Paul II. As long as women are associated with femininity, motherhood, and the work of production, while men are associated with headship, these roles in the church will be conceived of dualistically. This gendered conception of production and representation undermines ecclesial solidarity exemplified in Vatican II ecclesiology that emphasizes the church as the people of God and Body of Christ.

While feminists have made compelling arguments for the ordination of women,[25] and many Christian churches practice the ordination of women, the focus on ordination alone does not address the larger ecclesiological problem how gender and power are conceived. Women exercise power in the sanctuary movement both in ways that conform to the gender identity (i.e., the nurturing work) prescribed by the church and resist it (i.e., deciding to declare sanctuary and persuading the pastor). In the example highlighted in this chapter, lay women exercise agency through leading sanctuary discernment and sanctuary practices, thus resisting a hierarchical, patriarchal structure of the church. Their agency, however, is expressed within a context marked by an androcentric ecclesiology and cultural norms around gender, production, and representation. Rather than placing women in positions of hierarchically structured authority, sanctuary calls forth an ecclesiology that models solidarity within the church, marked by power-sharing fostered through mutual vulnerability and ongoing encounter.

---

24. Tina Beattie, "Transforming Time: The Maternal Church and the Pilgrimage of Faith," in *Pope Francis, Evangelii Gaudium, and the Renewal of the Church*, ed. Duncan Dormor and Alana Harris (Mahwah, NJ: Paulist Press, 2017), 86.

25. See, for example, *Women and Ordination in the Christian Churches: International Perspectives*, ed. Ian Jones, Kristy Thorpe, and Janet Wootton (London: T&T Clark, 2008).

By actively participating in sanctuary, women exercise leadership in their churches that may exclude them either formally or informally through theological constructions of gender. Their actions also reveal barriers to institutional commitment and invite transformation of ecclesial structures. Specifically, practices of solidarity create a space for the church to become an embodied expression of sanctuary. This transformation does not come from a top-down movement but from the church becoming decentered in ongoing encounters with those seeking sanctuary.

The gendered dynamics of power and representation were more pronounced in hierarchically structured churches, but they can be observed across denominational differences. The most significant factor I observed in how congregations discerned, declared, and practiced sanctuary is the experience or perception of risk and how that was addressed as a community. One's position and identity, particularly one's immigration status, shapes personal and congregational risk, inviting a reflection on power as part of the discernment process around sanctuary. However, I found that some congregations were more discerning around the ethical dimensions of risk than others.

Power, Representation, and Risk

I met Christina[26] one afternoon at a small church where she is pastor. She invited her colleague, Ana, a lay staff member of the church to join us. When I asked Christina and Ana about what led them to declare sanctuary, Christina told me the story of her congregation and her journey to become its pastor. Her church has always been at the service of immigrants—from the German and Irish immigrants who settled in her community in the early part of the twentieth century to the Latinx immigrants in the latter part of that century to the present day. Her life prepared her to lead an immigrant church. As an immigrant herself, she knows what it is like to leave her country and build life in

---

26. Names changed for anonymity.

a different culture and language. Her faith, rooted in a sense of radical dependency on God's grace, has been a source of strength and purpose in her journey. She was clear that the congregation's sanctuary declaration came "in God's time" and is part of "God's plan." Reflecting on her call to ordained ministry, she said:

> When I let go of my will, after I heard my call get much clearer many years later and I let go, I really understood that I was to do God's will . . . and that everything that you do should be in prayer and discernment because it's with God and we're humans. So we're going to still make decisions of our own and then maybe trip and fall, you know . . .[27]

Reflecting on the congregation's process of declaring sanctuary, she continued, "But I really feel that God's hand, God's blueprint, was for us to do this as we are, as small as we are, as tired as we are sometimes from going to point a and b . . . and sometimes we feel we can't do it. But it is God's will."[28]

Christina's account of her congregation's process of discerning and declaring sanctuary differed from the other people I interviewed. The overt theological language was striking, particularly the insistence on their sanctuary process as a response to God's plan and God's will. Her conviction that God was guiding the process and the timing of their declaration was reflected in her definition of sanctuary.

> When you think of a sanctuary, you think of the sacred space, this calming protection under God, you know, and a sanctified place where God is, where love is, where protection, where peace is. I mean that's what sanctuary means to us, you know. . . . So God had everything to do with it at every moment, I believe.[29]

Another notable aspect of this congregation's process of discerning and declaring sanctuary was their emphasis on creating a visible symbol

---

27. Interview with sanctuary participant, October 28, 2018.
28. Interview with sanctuary participant, October 28, 2018.
29. Interview with sanctuary participant, October 28, 2018.

of their sanctuary commitment for public display. The logo featured a cross with the word sanctuary embedded in its shape. They placed it in the center of a large sign with a scriptural passage, "Come to me all you who are weary, and I will give you rest." It was important to Christina and Ana that I see the sign and hear the story of its creation. For them, it represented a courageous public commitment, a lengthy discernment process over their identity as a community, and ultimately a covenant with God to be a sanctuary.

Christina emphasized the inclusiveness of their discernment, insisting that it was not the pastor's decision to declare sanctuary. The congregation went through a three-month discernment process that sought to include everyone's voice in the vote to declare sanctuary. Christina wanted to ensure the inclusivity of the process because of the specific risks her community faced in publicly declaring themselves as sanctuary:

> It wasn't just, oh, we're going to be a sanctuary congregation because we should. No, because there was a big risk and there's still a risk. And the risk is that many members, some members of our congregation, they're undocumented. So to put up a sign in the front of the church that says sanctuary, what would that entail? We went through all of those conversations, you know, and we decided, "Let's do it," and "We're going to take a risk."[30]

Christina named her fear that immigration enforcement would enter their worship space on Sunday and start detaining members of the congregation. She worried that they do not have an emergency plan to protect undocumented members of the community. Unlike other congregations in the city, she said, they do not have a lot of professionals, such as attorneys or people with wealth and connections, to navigate the legal system. So they have developed a partnership with an upper-middle-class congregation who has agreed to provide

---

30. Interview with sanctuary participant, October 28, 2018.

support, as needed. Christina named this as a source of security as she considers the risks her congregation is taking to be a public sanctuary.

This congregation, in many ways, offers a contrast to most congregations I studied. Christina was the only person who talked about the immigration status of church members in their discernment of risk. The risk of exposing undocumented immigrants or mixed-status families is an obvious barrier to public participation in sanctuary. Intersecting with immigration status are the realities of class, race, and ethnicity that shape one's power and vulnerability. This is one of the reasons leaders in the sanctuary movement and New Sanctuary Movement have struggled to achieve the inclusion of immigrant voices, despite their stated desire to be in solidarity with migrants.

Sociologist Grace Yukich names the lack of immigrant participation in the New Sanctuary Movement as one of its biggest weaknesses. She points to a number of reasons the New Sanctuary Movement has had little success recruiting immigrants. As a social movement, it reflects the style of its majority white upper-class members, with an emphasis on census-building and slow deliberation, which could be a source of frustration for communities used to a swifter model of decision-making. This, in addition to a language barrier, disempowered non-English speaking migrants and made them less likely to participate in public expressions of the movement.[31]

Yukich also suggests that the political aims of the movement were not as apparent to immigrant communities as were the charitable aspects. The North Americans who participated in the sanctuary movement of the 1980s took for granted that the goals of sanctuary included structural and long-term changes that would significantly benefit immigrants. However, she suggests:

> Despite New Sanctuary's attempts to highlight sanctuary as a movement strategy seeking widespread political and religious change, many of the people they tried to recruit viewed it as

31. Grace Yukich, *One Family under God: Immigration Politics and Progressive Religion in America* (Oxford University Press, 2013), 151–54.

"stepping up" only for certain immigrants, as helping them—as a form of charity. New Sanctuary congregations were seen as protectors, privileged and empowered to give aid to needy individuals, rather than as challengers of the system as a whole.[32]

If this is the case, it is not clear that the benefits to immigrants outweigh the risks of participating in the sanctuary movement. Yukich has argued that the perception that sanctuary is about charity has enabled churches to decide who gets sanctuary and who does not. This contributes to a problematic reinforcement of public perception that separates migrants into categories of deserving and undeserving of compassion. The New Sanctuary Movement's emphasis on helping "innocent" mixed status families reinforces the narrative that some migrants are deviant, dangerous, or undesirable—namely those who are "Muslims, black immigrants, single people, the unemployed . . ."[33]

Power and Representation in Migrant Testimony

Serin Houston and Charlotte Morse argue that the rhetoric surrounding the extraordinariness of migrant suffering as well as the ordinariness of certain migrant families have reinforced exclusion.[34] Migrant testimony has been a key aspect in shaping this powerful rhetoric. Central to the sanctuary movement of the 1980s and today, migrant testimony allows the church or the public to hear the story of a few migrants or refugees as representatives of a larger reality sanctuary seeks to address. In the 1980s, refugee stories of violence and oppression served as a critical tool for building the sanctuary movement and shifting the public understanding of the political situation in El Salvador and

---

32. Yukich, *One Family under God*, 151.

33. Grace Yukich, "Constructing the Model Immigrant: Movement Strategy and Immigrant Deservingness in the New Sanctuary Movement," *Social Problems* 60, no. 3 (2013): 302–20, at 315.

34. Serin Houston and Charlotte Morse, "The Ordinary and Extraordinary: Producing Migrant Inclusion and Exclusion in US Sanctuary Movements," *Studies in Social Justice* 11, no. 1 (2017): 27–47.

Guatemala.[35] Today, stories of family separation and deportation terror generate sympathy among churches and the wider public. One pastor I interviewed described migrant testimony as a "pastoral strategy" meant to generate sympathy for migrants and motivate the congregation to participate in their sanctuary commitment.

While several people I interviewed described hearing a "migrant in the pulpit" as a turning point for their involvement in sanctuary, the practice raises significant questions around representation. By elevating certain stories over others, it can reinforce polarizing rhetoric that not only excludes certain groups but also fails to address the systemic issues driving the dynamics of immigration and deportation. So, even if the intention behind migrant testimony is to motivate churches to resist unjust immigration policy, the practice can unintentionally reinforce the interests of those who benefit from the current economic and political structure that contributes to the oppression of migrants. In her critical analysis of migrant testimony in the sanctuary movement, Maria Elena Vargas argues that migrants were lifted up as deserving of sanctuary by their ability to appeal to a white, upper-class, Christian audience. "Tellability in religious context is constructed through social relations beyond the individual refugee and onto the Christian group membership. Thus, no matter how heart-wrenching and profound a story can be, its tellability is measured on its ability to evoke empathy from a faith-based audience."[36] Vargas points out how this construction excludes migrants who fall outside a particular script that appeals to the North American Christian audience.

On the other hand, some migrants have named the practice of testimony as a way to exercise agency. Elvira Arellano, an immigrant from Mexico who took sanctuary in a Chicago church in 2006 in order to avoid separation from her son, born in the United States, made her

35. Coutin, *Culture of Protest*.

36. Maria Elena Vargas, "Ghostly Others: Limiting Constructions of Deserving Subjects in Asylum Claims and Sanctuary Protection," *Journal of International Women's Studies* 21, no. 7 (2020): 77–90, Gale Academic OneFile, at link.gale.com/apps/doc/A640513174/AONE?u=usfca_gleeson&sid=AONE&xid=75ae34c9.

story public as a political strategy, "I wanted to talk about what was happening in my case in particular and to call attention . . . to what is going on . . . and ask what we want to do about it. I wanted to give us a voice."[37] Marta Caminero-Santangelo recognizes the strategic power of testimony as a way for undocumented migrants to exercise agency in a political context that renders them voiceless. At the same time, she highlights the complexity of agency in this context by reflecting on *testimonio* as a strategy for entering the public sphere. She argues that *testimonio* is a "highly mediated artifact,"[38] because it communicates truth in a way that anticipates how the hearer will receive the message with empathy. Caminero-Santangelo documents several examples of migrant narratives as expressions of agency but in an "impure" form because of the mediation. She argues, "But if *testimonio* provides a potential platform by which the subaltern can indeed speak, the very condition of subalternity generally necessitates the assistance of others in order to be made hearable."[39]

The church can serve as a mediator of migrant agency by providing a listening context that is not bound to the limited framework

37. D. Terry, "The New Sanctuary Movement," *Hispanic* (August 2007): 42–45, quoted in Marta Caminero-Santangelo, "Religious Rhetoric, Undocumented Migrants and the New Sanctuary Movement in the United States," in *Sanctuary Practices in International Perspectives: Migration, Citizenship and Social Movements*, ed. Randy Lippert and Sean Rehaag (New York: Routledge, 2012), 43.

38. Marta Caminero-Santangelo, *Documenting the Undocumented: Latino/a Narratives and Social Justice in the Era of Operation Gatekeeper* (Gainesville: University Press of Florida, 2016), 153.

39. Caminero-Santangelo, *Documenting the Undocumented*, 152. Caminero-Santangelo incorporates the language of subaltern in reference to Gayatri Spivak's highly influential essay "Can the Subaltern Speak?" Spivak demonstrates that once the subaltern's voice is amplified by institutions of power (i.e., the academy), they are no longer subaltern. Spivak's essay ultimately offers a critique of the academic field of postcolonial studies for attempting to speak for the subaltern. This critique points to the agency of the subaltern and the inability of the academy to listen. See Gayatri Chakravorty Spivak, "Can the Subaltern Speak?," rev. ed., from the "History" chapter of "Critique of Postcolonial Reason," in *Can the Subaltern Speak?: Reflections on the History of an Idea*, ed. Rosalind Morris (New York: Columbia University Press, 2010), 21–78.

of belonging based on nationhood. This can play an important role in amplifying migrant interests in the public sphere.[40] This requires decentering the dominant identities in the church to hear the voices of migrants define sanctuary in light of their experiences and goals. In this way, it becomes a concrete expression of the preferential option for the marginalized, acknowledging the epistemological privilege of the poor in the language of liberation theology.

More recent developments in liberation theology have resisted the overgeneralization or "mystification" of the marginalized by challenging the homogenous category of the "poor" by giving more attention to intersecting oppressions and identities related to race, sexuality, and gender.[41] Ivan Petrella responds to what he describes as the first generation of liberation theologians' inability "to grasp fully the situation of colonial heterogeneity lying underneath the 'poor' it sought to address."[42] Postcolonial theories have been helpful in this project as it attends to the complex power relations embedded in multiple identities and breaks down binary thinking about oppressor-oppressed. Marcella Althaus-Reid has argued that it is not enough for liberation theology to privilege the perspective of the poor using traditional theological methodologies that aim for coherence and erase complexity. Althaus-Reid draws upon postcolonial and queer theology to disrupt the romanticized, homogenized "poor" produced by Western epistemologies.[43] She models a way to honor the epistemological privilege of the marginalized not in an abstract way but in a way that *decenters*

---

40. This argument is developed by Pierrette Hondagneu-Sotelo in *God's Heart Has No Borders: How Religious Activists Are Working for Immigrant Rights* (Berkeley: University of California Press, 2008), as well as by Marta Caminero-Santagelo, "The Voice of the Voiceless: Religious Rhetoric, Undocumented Immigrants, and the New Sanctuary Movement in the United States," in Lippert and Rehaag, *Sanctuary Practices*, 92–105.

41. See Ivan Petrella, ed. *Latin American Liberation Theology: The Next Generation* (Maryknoll, NY: Orbis, 2005).

42. Petrella, *Latin American Liberation Theology*, xvii.

43. Marcella Althaus-Reid, *From Feminist Theology to Indecent Theology* (London: SCM, 2004)

the dominant perspective. In this way, the margins move to the center as the site of resistance.

Analyzing the practice of migrant testimony from this perspective prompts a reflection not so much on the intention but its practical effects. Does the congregation interpret the testimony through their own categories, or does the testimony disrupt their thinking in a radical way? Is the congregation willing to be decentered to make space for deep listening, critical engagement, and dialogue with those who have been oppressed? Kwok Pui Lan argues that these actions are the basis of solidarity because they allow us to overcome ignorance and indifference toward the other.[44] But this kind of solidarity does not happen quickly or easily. It involves ongoing contact, attention to the lived realities of those on the margins. And like any meaningful relationship, it involves risk.

Risk was evoked frequently as a significant factor in discernment around sanctuary. Christina's congregation identified the risk of exposing undocumented members to immigration enforcement. Christina also understood the risk of her congregation with respect to their limited economic and political power. However, since most congregations interviewed for this study did not have large migrant population, they defined risk more in terms of community identity, whether religious or political. As noted in the last chapter, sanctuary leaders were concerned that a public declaration would divide their community along political lines. The discussion of risk often involved assuaging members that the congregation would not be breaking the law by harboring undocumented immigrants, thus distinguishing physical sanctuary from sanctuary as accompaniment, education, and advocacy.

The absence of a critical analysis of power, risk, and representation reinforces barriers to solidarity in the sanctuary movement. If congregations are to align their sanctuary practices with a sanctuary theology rooted in solidarity, they need resources to discern risk. Drawing upon

---

44. Kwok Pui Lan, "Margins and the Changing Spatiality of Power," in *Still at the Margins: Biblical Scholarship Fifteen Years after Voices from the Margin*, ed. R. S. Sugirtharajah (New York: T&T Clark, 2008): 114–27.

Christian ethics and feminist theory, Sharon Welch offers an approach to risk that is relevant to the context of sanctuary.

A Feminist Ethic of Risk

Writing on ethics of deterrence during the nuclear arms race of the 1980s, Welch addresses disillusionment among white middle-class activists, which she argues stems from how they frame success. "Taking as a norm of power the ability to the political and economic establishment to meet its goals, middle class activists often become trapped in cultural despair."[45] She observes a contrast between these activists and African American women who have demonstrated the power of incremental change and the importance of accountability without guarantee of success. Inspired by African American novelists who define "responsible action within the limits of bounded power," Welch describes an ethic of risk which recognizes "that we cannot guarantee decisive changes in the near future or even our lifetime."[46]

Welch distinguishes the ethic of risk from an ethic of control. Reinforced by a belief in an omnipotent God and confidence in one's economic and political power, an ethic of control predetermines the outcome of social change and defines the parameters of successful activism. When its adherents do not achieve their goals, this ethic can not only lead to cynicism or stagnation but can become a barrier to solidarity. "If control is the norm, then responsible action for justice is a contradiction in terms."[47]

Control was not the norm in Christina's declaration of sanctuary. She stressed the inclusive process of discernment around shared risk, not wanting to claim the authority to declare or represent the community's sanctuary commitment. In her experience, it was God's plan, God's authority, that guided their discernment. And it was a co-constructed visual symbol that represented the congregation's stance on

---

45. Sharon Welch, *A Feminist Ethic of Risk* (Minneapolis: Fortress Press, 2000), 103.

46. Welch, *Feminist Ethic of Risk*, 45–46.

47. Welch, *Feminist Ethic of Risk,* 104.

sanctuary. In this case, the congregation declared sanctuary in the face of risk, knowing that people in their own community would remain vulnerable. The declaration itself was a celebration of success. Welch claims that small successes are important for activist communities because they create a communal matrix of resistance. She argues:

> The extent to which an action is an appropriate response to the needs of others is constituted as much by the possibilities it creates as by its immediate results. Responsible action does not mean one individual resolving the problems of others. It is, rather, participation in a communal work, laying the groundwork for the creative response of people in the present and in the future.[48]

However, as a majority white upper-class movement, sanctuary reflects assumptions of people who experience relative economic and political power and manifest some characteristics Welch associates with an ethic of control. Consider how the election of Donald Trump fueled the New Sanctuary Movement. Sanctuary leaders expressed shock, rage, and a sense of unprecedented urgency upon Trump's election. This was the impetus for many congregations to go public with their sanctuary commitment. It has been pointed out that these experiences were common among white middle-class people but not shared by people of color, who saw the election of Trump as an expression of white supremacy and xenophobia that they experience on a regular basis.[49]

Guided by an ethic of control, some sanctuary leaders struggle to take risks. Fear over legal consequences, economic costs, and loss of identity emerge as congregations discern action around sanctuary. Welch describes how an ethic of control undermines solidarity, arguing that it eliminates the possibility of mutual transformation that emerges when multiple perspectives are engaged. She draws upon

---

48. Welch, *Feminist Ethic of Risk,* 75.

49. Kelly Brown Douglas suggests, "The ascendency of Trump to the presidency is about nothing less than whiteness standing its ground to protect America's Anglo-Saxon mythic self with a law-and-order agenda and wall-building promises" ("Trump's America: What Will We Do about It?," in *Faith and Resistance in the Age of Trump,* ed. Miguel de la Torre [Maryknoll, NY: Orbis, 2017]).

Jürgen Habermas's communicative ethics to argue that the goal of ethical action cannot be assumed through universal norms but must emerge discursively. Following Seyla Benhabib, Welch argues that the goal is not achieved through rational argumentation but by concrete encounters with others.

Emphasizing encounter, Welch insists that the kind of mutual transformation that allows a shared vision to emerge does not happen simply through conversation. Welch argues, "Conversation alone is not enough. Emancipatory conversations are the fruit of work together, the result of alterations in relationships between groups. In work we create as much as we affirm the rational principle of shared humanity."[50] She goes on to describe shared life together as involving material life—including the messy action often relegated to the private sphere—cooking, building, working, and child-rearing. Similarly, *Mujerista* theologian Ada Maria Isasi-Diaz articulates the centrality of everyday lived experiences in understanding another as the basis of solidarity. She describes the concept of *lo cotidiano* or "the space–time and place–which we face daily, but it also refers to how we face it and to our way of dealing with it."[51]

Solidarity, in this view, cannot be achieved through listening to migrants' stories without entering into their lifeworld, working alongside them to realize together what sanctuary looks like. Accompaniment that involves this level of accountability and shared life becomes central to the work of sanctuary. Recall Mary, whose experience of solidarity was not assumed but emerged through sharing her life and participating in the life of the sanctuary family. She discovered a sense of kinship through mutual vulnerability, through taking up the messy work of sanctuary.

This experience provides a way forward as churches discern risk. It allows sanctuary participants to celebrate small incremental changes

---

50. Welch, *Feminist Ethic of Risk*, 135.

51. Ada Maria Isasi-Diaz, "Mujerista Discourse: A Platform for Latinas' Subjugated Knowledge," in *Decolonizing Epistemologies: Latina/o Theology and Philosophy*, ed. Ada Maria Isasi-Díaz and Eduardo Mendieta (New York: Fordham University Press, 2011): 44–67, at 49.

and hold onto a vision of justice despite obstacles. For Welch, it also offers a source of sustaining joy:

> The fundamental risk constitutive of this ethic is the decision to care and to act although there are no guarantees of success. Such action requires immense daring and enables deep joy. It is an ethos in sharp contrast to the ethos of cynicism that often accompanies a recognition of the depth and persistence of evil.[52]

If we consider sanctuary this way, it becomes clear that it is cocreated by relationships of mutual vulnerability and risk. It is not something the church offers to the migrant "other" but rather something that emerges in sharing stories, walking together, and building solidarity gradually through shared life. Gemma Tulud Cruz underscores risk-taking for the common good as a concrete expression of Catholic social thought:

> It is not easy to give up some of our rights or comforts for the sake of the other as the Catholic ethic on common good dictates. Neither is it easy to practice solidarity or say *mi casa su casa* to anyone or everyone, especially in this day and age that is characterized by uncertainty, insecurity, and violence. But risk we must, because risk itself is a fundamental virtue in Catholic ethical perspectives.[53]

An Ecclesiology of Embodied Solidarity

The concrete work of accompaniment—sharing in the material realities of marginalized people—provides a basis for solidarity. Migrant testimony offers the opportunity for transformative encounter when it is situated in ongoing contact that involves shared work and mutual vulnerability. Though often relegated to the private sphere, the work of

---

52. Welch, *Feminist Ethic of Risk*, 68.
53. Gemma Tulud Cruz, "Toward an Ethic of Risk: CST and Immigration Reform," *Studies in Christian Ethics* 24, no. 3 (August 2011): 294–310, at 308.

accompaniment should inform the public engagement, challenging a rigid distinction between the public and private work of sanctuary. In this context, accompaniment means that concrete practices of sanctuary should inform the discernment around risk and representation. Attention to embodied practices of sanctuary reveal the "recipients" of sanctuary as the producers of it. Sanctuary is a decentering practice when it emerges out of shared risk and mutual transformation.

Power dynamics in the church that perpetuate a separation of the work of production and work of representation limit the sanctuary movement's ability to achieve solidarity. An ecclesiology of sanctuary, then, needs to be informed by an analysis of power with respect to gender, race, ethnicity, and immigration status. In what follows, I will highlight some ecclesiologies that have emphasized power-sharing and solidarity within the church, as I am convinced that this is a prerequisite for extending solidarity toward the marginalized.

Johann Baptist Metz has effectively argued that the church can only exercise its prophetic function when it manifests the justice it announces in the world. He connects the church's complacency with injustice with passivity among the baptized. A privatized bourgeois expression of Christianity goes hand in hand with a paternalistic ecclesial structure and theology that encourages the laity to be passive consumers of religion. Metz contrasts this hierarchical model of the church with the ecclesial base communities that were emerging out of Latin America during the 1970s and '80s. Metz longed to see some form of ecclesial base communities replace the bourgeois churches of Europe, but he recognized that it would be a movement of lay people exercising their subjectivity as members of the Body of Christ. "The transition from a paternalistic church 'taking care of the people' to a mature church 'of the people' does not simply come from above; in fact, it cannot come from above at all."[54]

Pope Francis has acknowledged the problem of "excessive clericalism" in some contexts that marginalizes the laity from decision-making

---

54. Johann Baptist Metz, *The Emergent Church: The Future of Christianity in a Postbourgeois World*, trans. Peter Mann (New York: Crossroad, 1981), 85.

in the church. He presents this as a significant pastoral challenge, recognizing that lay people are "the vast majority of the people of God"
and that many of them have a "deeply-rooted sense of community."
Francis acknowledges the particular marginalization of women from
formal leadership and invites pastors and theologians to reimagine
ways to integrate women's voices into the decision-making processes
of the church. While Francis does not question the church's exclusion
of women from ordained ministry, he challenges clerical attitudes that
elevate ordained members of the church above others.[55] Elsewhere, he
has instructed pastors to stay rooted in relationship with the people
they serve, "to be shepherds with the smell of sheep."[56] While Francis
has rejected clericalism and embraced a consultative-conciliar model
of church, some have argued that Francis does not go far enough to
provide an alternative theological vision for the inclusion of women in
church leadership.[57] Feminist theologians have demonstrated the connection between patriarchy and clericalism, which have both prevented
the church from embodying Francis's Christ-centered ecclesiology that
grounds all ministry in baptism.

In her feminist ecclesiology, Elisabeth Schüssler Fiorenza retrieves
and reconstructs an alternative model of church found in early Christian practices. Before church leadership roles were formalized through
ordination, authority in the church operated nonhierarchically and
counterculturally. Against the backdrop of a patriarchal family and
social structure, early Christians saw themselves as *ekklesia*, a community of equals. Schüssler Fiorenza argues that this subversive model of
church was gradually erased by a patriarchal reading of history, which
now necessitates a hermeneutic of suspicion to retrieve the original,

55. Pope Francis, EG, 102–9.

56. Pope Francis, Address to the World's Priests at the Chrism Mass on Holy Thursday, March 28, 2013, at http://www.vatican.va/content/francesco/en/homilies
/2013/documents/papa-francesco_20130328_messa-crismale.html, accessed on July
1, 2020.

57. Catholic Women Speak Network, *Catholic Women Speak: Bringing Our Gifts to
the Table* (Mahwah, NJ: Paulist Press, 2015); Tina Beattie, "Transforming Time: The
Maternal Church and the Pilgrimage of Faith," in Dormor and Harris, *Pope Francis*.

more egalitarian model of discipleship. Like Metz, Schüssler Fiorenza connects justice in the church with the church's ability to announce the "dangerous memory" of Jesus as a liberator of the oppressed.[58]

Similarly, Letty Russell constructs a feminist ecclesiology through retrieval of early Christian practices. She argues that the early self-understanding of the church as *koinonia,* or Christ-centered communion, enabled them to practice hospitality with the marginalized, which she lifts up as a central characteristic of the church. Using the metaphor of a round table, Russell emphasizes Jesus's radically inclusive practice of table fellowship and the church's call to be space where everyone is welcome. The round table metaphor also applies to leadership in the church. Russell sees clericalism as a hindrance for cultivating a round table church and argues for a transformation of how we think about ministry rather than inserting women into the same model, "the clerical structures continue to reinforce structures of hierarchy and domination, whether or not the particular clergyperson is male or female."[59] Specifically, she points to a "functional" model of ministry that is not so much focused on ontological qualities of an ordained person but one that focuses on the particular gifts of a minister in light of the mission of the church.[60] The emphasis on praxis is particularly helpful in resisting the gendered separation of the work of sanctuary and the public declaration of sanctuary.

By situating ministry in history, guided by a feminist hermeneutic, Russell and Schüssler Fiorenza offer insights on how the church can embody the solidarity it proclaims and inform practices of hospitality in the concrete experience of accompaniment with the marginalized. The emphasis on practice is key because subjectivity and agency can emerge in invisible and sometimes surprising ways.[61] Sanctuary

---

58. Elizabeth Schüssler-Fiorenza, *In Memory of Her: A Feminist Theological Reconstruction of Christian Origins* (London: SCM Press, 1983).

59. Letty Russell, *Church in the Round: Feminist Interpretation of the Church* (Louisville: Westminster/John Knox Press, 1993), 51.

60. Russell, *Church in the Round.*

61. Mary McClintock Fulkerson has demonstrated this in her analysis of agency among women in conservative Christian churches who do not identify as feminists.

is co-constructed in concrete practices of solidarity, through mutual sharing of vulnerability.

In this chapter, I have argued that those who do the work of accompaniment should inform the institutional identity of the church as a sanctuary. This invites nonhierarchical experiences of the church as *koinonia* and *ekklesia*, recognizing that these experiences may emerge in different forms and in surprising ways. Being rooted in solidarity allows the church to practice an ethic of risk, extending solidarity to those who are struggling for justice. The next chapter will highlight a radically embodied way of practicing solidarity. It will lift up a particular church community who gives expression to sanctuary through opening its doors to unhoused people and offering a space for sacred sleep.[62] This practice of sanctuary invites us to consider the significance of sacred space, allowing the world, in all its messiness, to enter and transform the church.

She uses poststructuralist theory to describe how meaning is always embedded and situational, complicating the very notion of "women's experience" in feminist theology. See Mary McClintock Fulkerson, *Changing the Subject: Women's Discourses and Feminist Theology* (Minneapolis: Fortress Press, 1994).

62. The Gubbio Project describes their mission as providing sacred sleep, community, and sanctuary through opening doors of worship spaces so unhoused people can sleep in the space. See their website https://www.thegubbioproject.org/.

Chapter 4

Sanctuary as Sacramental Praxis

situate myself near the door of the church so I can greet people as they enter and leave the space. As a volunteer, my role is to ritualize hospitality—listening to people if they want to talk, letting people know with a smile and hello that everyone is welcome to enter the space. A diverse group of people come and go freely; there are no questions or intake forms. People bring their possessions in overflowing bags or shopping carts. Some bring their dogs. Often, especially upon leaving, they will dip their fingers in the holy water and make the sign of the cross.

The space, designed by Franciscan brother Adrian Weaver in 1902 and rebuilt after the 1906 earthquake, has a large, ornately painted domed ceiling and arched stained glass windows depicting stories from the Christian tradition.[1] Side altars dedicated to Catholic saints are surrounded by candles and incense. The Catholic, Franciscan-inspired parish of St. Boniface describes itself as an "oasis in the Tenderloin." The Gubbio Project, an interfaith nonprofit that provides sacred sleep

---

1. Anne Bloomfield and Michael Corbett, *National Register of Historic Places Nomination Form for the Uptown Tenderloin Historic District* (May 5, 2008). Nomination confirmed by the Keeper of the National Register, February 5, 2009.

in the worship space, describes itself as a "sanctuary," a place of safety for unhoused people to rest.

The multicultural parish of St. Boniface offers Mass in Vietnamese, Tagalog, Spanish, and English. Each weekday at noon, Mass is said in English. During this hour, the hybridity of the space, as a parish and as Gubbio, is pronounced. The wooden pews in the front of the church that are always reserved for quiet prayer and reflection are occupied by a dozen or so participants in the Mass. The pews in the back remain occupied by guests of Gubbio, some of whom seem to observe or participate in the Mass, while many sleep, continue to sort their possessions, or quietly look at their cell phones.

Before the Mass, I watch as a middle-aged woman of Asian descent tends to the space in front. She changes flowers, lights candles, and genuflects each time she passes the tabernacle. She occasionally interacts with the Franciscan brothers who minister at Gubbio. At the same time, an African American woman wearing a Gubbio T-shirt tends to the space in the back. She lights incense, wipes down pews, and checks on guests. She knows them by name. I am struck by the parallel activities of these women, who in different ways, create and maintain the beauty of the space.

Far from superfluous, the cultivation of beauty has a central role in allowing the space to function as both oasis and sanctuary. These women, who might lack the visibility of the formal authority figure, are the agents, perhaps even ministers, of the sacred in the space. In the front of the church, the priest presides over the celebration, signaling when to sit and stand and speak. In the back, a hospitality monitor gently but firmly reminds people to be quiet or occasionally asks people to leave.

Through months of participant observation and formal interviews with over twenty-five volunteers and staff, I became aware of a different kind of authority that emerges from the space itself. Gubbio staff and volunteers readily comment on the power of being in a church. The space itself influences behavior, allowing Gubbio to practice a low-barrier, harm-reduction approach to their work of providing hospitality among unhoused people. The space, in this sense, promotes quiet, peacefulness, respect, which allows Gubbio to be a sanctuary for the unhoused.

At the same time, sustained observation and interviews reveal multiple conceptions of the space, some of which resist traditional notions of church. Volunteers and staff conceive Gubbio as both a church and nonchurch. For many, the church as an expression of institutionalized religion represents exclusion, hierarchy, dogmatism, is rejected and resisted by Gubbio. In contrast, Gubbio cultivates an openness, inclusion, and sense of the sacred that resonates with the spiritual lives of many people I interviewed.

This chapter will explore some of the articulated dimensions of spirituality and religion that emerged in interviews with volunteers and staff. Situating these themes within theological and sociological discourse on religious identity in a secular age, I will argue two things. First, the expressive individualism that promotes disaffiliation with religion in the quest for spiritual authenticity has a social dimension and can lead to meaningful and motivating experiences of community. Second, the rejection of religious institutions does not mean religion ceases to have authority. Rather, religion's authority emerges through embodiment of its deepest beliefs and values. This context reinforces the need for an ecclesiology of embodied practices that reveal the content of faith. In other words, Gubbio is powerful because people with various experiences of religion can recognize the embodiment of the Gospel that they expect and desire to see in a Christian church. The sacramental praxis draws people into the beauty of the space and its beauty de-centers relationships, allowing sanctuary to emerge.

Church beyond Religion

Spirituality in a Post-Secular Context

> I think of myself being a very spiritual person; it's not necessarily my preference, the faith. I am interfaith. I've been interfaith for a while. I do believe it's very important, that spirituality. It plays a big role in the environment also. I think it feeds off that. You're down, you stare at people praying, you have Mass come in every day, and people are praying and praising God. That's power. I think it affects the whole environment to a certain extent. I think

it does. I think it keeps a good balance in the midst of all this stuff you're going through. All this trauma, lots of trauma of varying levels.[2]

When I asked staff and volunteers to share what drew them to Gubbio, they frequently shared their faith story and identity. The fact that this question, which does not mention faith, religion, or spirituality, prompted such a reflection is itself worth noting. It is also worth noting that the majority of interviewees distinguished spirituality from religion, and a number of them rejected the latter. The quote above highlights a number of recurring themes that reflect larger trends in North American religiosity. Those who identify as "nothing in particular" when asked about religious affiliation, sometimes described as religious "nones," are on the rise. At the same time, Catholics and mainstream Protestants overall have shown a decline over the past ten years.[3] The category of interfaith, though not frequently used to describe one's identity, emerged as an important theme when people recounted their spiritual journey of leaving a particular religion, usually Christianity, discovering elements of other religions, and embracing some practices while rejecting others.

Robert Wuthnow describes the practice of "spiritual tinkering" prevalent among people in their twenties in the United States. Spiritual tinkering, which involves making choices about one's spirituality from multiple sources, is cultivated by a pluralistic culture that also values personal freedom. Spiritual tinkering, for some, involves church shopping, searching among many options within the "spiritual marketplace," before settling on a church. It may involve church hop-

2. Interview with Gubbio participant on April 8, 2020.

3. See the Pew Research Center on Religion in Public Life's Religious Landscape Survey 2014, at https://www.pewforum.org/2015/05/12/americas-changing-religious -landscape/, accessed June 25, 2020. More recently, a 2020 Gallup Poll revealed that for the first time since they began collecting data, the majority of people in the United States do not identify with a particular church or synagogue. Jeffrey Jones, "U.S. Church Membership Falls Below Majority for the First Time" (March 29, 2021), at https://news .gallup.com/poll/341963/church-membership-falls-below-majority-first-time.aspx.

ping, characterized by going back and forth among congregations and practices without settling on a single affiliation.[4]

In *Habits of the Heart*, the frequently cited study of democracy and middle-class culture in the United States, Robert Bellah and his colleagues noted the enduring trend of piecing together elements of religious belief and practice. Bellah uses the language of expressive individualism to describe the religious consciousness he observed when coauthoring *Habits* in 1985. "Expressive individualism holds that each person has a unique core of feeling and intuition that should unfold or be expressed if individuality is to be realized."[5] To illustrate, the authors cite a woman whose pseudonym has become associated with "spiritual but not religious." A young nurse in their study, Sheila Larson, describes, "I believe in God. I'm not a religious fanatic. I can't remember the last time I went to church. My faith has carried me a long way. It's Sheilaism. Just my own little voice."[6]

Within the framework of expressive individualism, one's personal faith should appeal to his or her sense of self over affiliation with a particular community or tradition. However, expressive individualism is not necessarily isolating, as recent sociology of religion demonstrates. Although young people are less likely to attend church regularly and less likely to have friends through a congregation, Wuthnow observes the importance of friendship in influencing one's choices around spirituality.[7] Similarly, Kelly Besecke challenges the idea that noninstitutional religion is individualistic, pointing out ways that nonaffiliated individuals connect around transcendent meaning through persistent communication about spirituality. By emphasizing the communicative dimension of religion, she highlights the power of religion on a

---

4. Robert Wuthnow, *After the Baby Boomers: How Twenty- and Thirty-Somethings Are Shaping the Future of American Religion* (Princeton: Princeton University Press, 2007), 112–35.

5. Robert Bellah, Richard Madsen, William Sullivan, Ann Swidler, and Steven Tipton, *Habits of the Heart*, 2nd ed. (University of California Press, 1996), 333–35.

6. Bellah et al., *Habits of the Heart*, 221.

7. Wuthnow, *After the Baby Boomers*, 135.

level that cannot be reduced to the individual or the institutional.[8] Richard Wood demonstrates how community organizing brings people together, shapes religious culture, and motivates social movements.[9]

Charles Taylor examines the significance of religion and spirituality beyond the question of affiliation and religious practice. In his seminal text *A Secular Age*, Charles Taylor debunks "subtraction theories" which, following Max Weber, assume religious belief and practice would decline as societies became more industrialized and modernized. For Taylor, the central question marking a secular age is this: "Why was it virtually impossible not to believe in God in, say, 1500 in our Western society, while in 2000 many of us find this not only easy, but even inescapable?"[10] Taylor addresses this question by describing "the sensed context in which we develop our beliefs" as the immanent frame.[11] While the immanent frame shares features of Weber's disenchanted worldview, wherein the modern person no longer experiences oneself as part of a predetermined natural order that discloses transcendence, it also resists such disenchantment. Taylor describes a persistent longing for transcendence, sometimes in a nostalgic desire for the immediate experience of God expressed in the awe-inspiring medieval cathedral.[12] He also describes the lure of immanence, particularly in the experience of nature or the sacraments, marked by a desire to experience oneself as part of something larger than the individual.[13]

The immanent frame pulls us in multiple directions, creating the possibility for diverse ways of relating to faith in a secular age. Taylor interprets expressivist individualism from this basic assumption, arguing, "The new framework has a strongly individualist component, but

8. Kelly Besecke "Seeing Invisible Religion: Religion as a Societal Conversation about Transcendent Meaning," *Sociological Theory* 23, no. 2 (January 1, 2005): 179–96.

9. Richard Wood "Religious Culture and Political Action," *Sociological Theory* 17, no. 3 (November 1999), 307–32.

10. Charles Taylor, *A Secular Age* (Cambridge, MA: Harvard University Press, 2007), 25.

11. Taylor, *A Secular Age*, 549.

12. Taylor, *A Secular Age,* 553.

13. Taylor, *A Secular Age,* 547.

this will not necessarily mean that the content will be individuating. Many people will find themselves joining extremely powerful religious communities. Because that's where many people's sense of the spiritual will lead them."[14]

Gubbio attests to Taylor's observation that there are multiple ways of relating to faith in a secular context of San Francisco. It also speaks to the longing for immanence that Taylor names, which I will return to later in the chapter as I explore the role of beauty in cultivating the sense of the sacred space. Interviews revealed a strong appeal to personal experience over religious authority in constructing one's spiritual identity. A number of people reported what Wuthnow describes as church shopping or hopping, searching among options for the right spiritual fit. Some settle into a congregation and some prefer to identify with a variety of congregations or faith traditions. And while this approach to spirituality locates authority in one's personal experience, there is an unmistakable longing for community among spiritual seekers at Gubbio.

This longing for community, notably, was not limited to people who reflect one's own social demographic or immediate social circle. Most staff and volunteers spoke of a desire for mutuality, solidarity, or connection with unhoused people. Some connected this desire to a personal or family experience of marginalization or trauma. I spoke to people who at some point had experienced homelessness, incarceration, or poverty. I spoke to people who observed family members experience mental illness, addiction, or homelessness. I also spoke to many people who did not experience these realities directly and felt a discomfort over their own privilege around housing and resources.

Many volunteers and staff cited their discomfort seeing unhoused people on the streets. The discomfort was expressed not only in terms of the dehumanizing conditions of street homelessness but also in terms of their own responses. Several confessed that they have walked by a person experiencing homelessness and avoided eye contact. One woman wrestled with guilt over working at a tech company that moved

14. Taylor, *A Secular Age*, 516.

into the Tenderloin and drove up housing prices. Nearly everyone I interviewed expressed a desire for a relationship with unhoused people that was mutually transformative, which seems to go beyond a desire for personal fulfillment.

The rejection of religious institutions was not simply motivated by a desire to carve out a spiritual identity that spoke to one's sense of self. It was not solely motivated by the perceived hypocrisy among religious leaders that violated one's ethic of authenticity. I also heard a desire for relationship at the heart of most people's stories—the kinds of relationships that would redeem the violence they saw in the rampant street homelessness of San Francisco but that would also lead to a personal transformation in relationship with unhoused people. A prevalent view was that highly structured institutions disallow the kinds of relationships that foster this transformation. There are parallels in how interviewees perceive churches and traditional homeless shelters. Both are viewed as bureaucratic, rule-bound, hierarchical, and exclusionary. Gubbio is the ultimate contrast. It is open to everyone. Rules are intentionally minimal and centered on mutual safety and respect for the atmosphere that cultivates sacred sleep. For people who have experienced religion as exclusionary or oppressive, Gubbio offers a place of healing.

Religion Hurts, Gubbio Redeems

"I mean, having grown up in a Roman Catholic background, I myself have had to go through a lot of things to release the pain and difficulty that came from that experience and upbringing as well. A lot of times things inside churches, or just being inside the church, can be very triggering. In a not-so-happy way."[15]

Several participants, like the woman quoted above, expressed the personal impact of negative experiences of religion. The sources of pain, frustration, or anger were described in various ways. The theme of hypocrisy was prominent. Even people who did not come from a Christian background or associate with Christianity had a sense of

---

15. Interview with Gubbio participant on April 3, 2020.

what the church was supposed to be and expressed disappointment or anger when it failed to live up to these expectations. A few people cited the scandal of clergy sexual abuse and the abuse of authority among bishops who covered it up. Most frequently disappointment and anger emerged through an experience of being excluded by the church because of one's identity, and this was particularly striking among those who identify as LGBTQ.

The openness of Gubbio, marked by low-barrier service and non-judgmental acceptance, offers a contrast experience for people who have been excluded from the church. I recall an interaction with a guest at Gubbio who tearfully expressed this experience. Now middle-aged, he was living on the streets after leaving home in his youth. His mother, a devout Catholic, rejected him after learning that he was gay. He wore a rosary around his neck and told me how much he loved resting in the church, being surrounded by images of Jesus and Mary and the saints. His faith was a source of comfort after his mother, with whom he never reconciled, died a few years ago.

Multiple staff members shared recurring observations like the one above. Contrasting the experience of not being safe in one's family or community with the experience of safety at Gubbio, one staff member noted:

> But there were so many people that, too, were crying during service, so many were queer and so many had mental health issues and they got rejected by their family for either being queer or for having mental health issues or for whatever other reason. Maybe they weren't that smart or [for] whatever reason, they kind of got cast out of the community. And that included getting cast out of church . . . especially gay folks. . . . I just can't tell you how important that was to be in the church.[16]

Coming to Gubbio as an unhoused guest seeking sleep and respite from the streets is different from those who come to Gubbio as

---

16. Interview with Gubbio participant on January 24, 2020.

a volunteer or staff member or a researcher like me. These positions, marked by different levels of power in society and the church space, cannot be disregarded. The parallels are noteworthy, however, among what I observed among some guests and what some volunteers and staff members describe in terms of the contrast experience at Gubbio that allowed them to experience the church differently, at least in that space and in that particular context.

One older man I interviewed discussed his faith journey and the important role of Gubbio in freeing him to discover a sense of spirituality in the church space. He described the important role of Catholicism in his past. He held onto the church despite experiencing a disconnect with high liturgy and the official church teaching that failed to recognize his marriage to a man. "We were outcasts," he described. Yet, from that experience on the periphery of the church, he was able to carve out alternative ways of belonging and leading in the church. He and his husband were leaders in a gay Catholic organization for a period of time. However, he expressed discomfort with the official liturgy and teachings of the church, creating a barrier to full participation. Gubbio creates a space for another experience:

> But the nature of the liturgy demands, I think if you're going to be honest, it demands a degree of participation that we're just not emotionally capable of at this point. So, the Creed, I can't say the Creed because I don't believe it. So that to me makes it difficult, very difficult. But on the other hand, when I go to [the church] for Gubbio, that's as spiritual as I've felt in years. I'm not sure why.[17]

With experiences of exclusion like those noted above, it comes as no surprise that participants experience an incompatibility with religion and the values that draw them to Gubbio—inclusion, acceptance, openness, and affirmation of everyone's dignity. Sociologists of religion have studied this on macro levels, noting that disaffiliated "nones" as-

---

17. Interview with Gubbio participant on April 8, 2020.

sociate religion with political conservatism, particularly surrounding issues such as gay marriage and abortion. Disaffiliation with religion flows from the image of religion as intolerant and exclusionary.[18] This sociological observation explains the frequent disassociation from religious institutions among participants. But it does not explain the draw to Gubbio or the sense of spirituality evoked by the church space.

In the next section, I reflect on this attraction to Gubbio in a post-secular context using Richard Kearney's concept of sacramental praxis. Exemplified by the life and thought of Dorothy Day, sacramental praxis reveals God's self-emptying love through radical openness toward the nonsovereign stranger. It makes faith visible and credible even when traditional notions of an all-powerful God and dogmatic religion have been rejected. Turning toward the sacramental, one is confronted with the role of beauty in the practice of sanctuary at Gubbio. Drawing upon the philosophies of Simone Weil and Elaine Scarry, I will demonstrate the relationship between beauty and justice, highlighting the decentering role of beauty that allows sanctuary to emerge.

Sacramental Praxis

Redemptive Beauty

When volunteers and staff expressed positive views of the church, it was generally around a person or community perceived to embody the Gospel. One woman described activist nuns and priests who she saw leading the sanctuary movement in the 1980s, another named Jesuits in college who taught her about social justice. Some people spoke in more general terms, pointing out that religion can inspire people to goodness. One person observed that religion has "staying power" in working with marginalized communities—when individuals, secular nonprofits, or state sponsored services leave, the faith communities

---

18. Robert Putnam, David E. Campbell, and Shaylyn Romney Garrett, *American Grace: How Religion Divides and Unites Us* (New York: Simon & Schuster, 2010).

stay. Charles Taylor recognizes this longing to see the embodiment of faith, even if faith cannot be grasped:

> The secular age is schizophrenic, or better, deeply cross-pressured. People seem at a safe distance from religion; and yet they are very moved to know that there are dedicated believers, like Mother Teresa. . . . It's as though many people who don't want to follow want nevertheless to hear the message of Christ, want it to be proclaimed out there.[19]

The staff and volunteers I interviewed were quick to point out hypocrisy in the church but equally eager to name exemplars of the faith. Four participants specifically named a former staff member at Gubbio as "Christlike," a "saint," one who exemplified the potential of religion for good. A volunteer remembers her:

> One day I'm in the closet again and some guy needed something for his feet. And the next thing I know there's [staff member] on the floor with the guy sitting on a chair and she's rubbing this ointment or lotion or whatever it was on his feet. A really grungy looking homeless guy, someone who most of us would walk around on the street. And there she was in front of him putting it up and down his lower leg, onto his ankle, onto his feet, between his toes, just a really intimate moment. And even get a little choked up recalling it because I'm like, "That is Christlike," and that just stuck with me.[20]

In this limited sample of San Franciscans, most of whom do not identify with Christianity, there was a remarkable consistency in their sense of what Christianity was supposed to be. Without using the language of the preferential option for the poor, people affirmed what liberation theologians have insisted—the church should be on the side of those who are impoverished and marginalized. One staff member

---

19. Taylor, *A Secular Age*, 727.
20. Interview with Gubbio participant on April 3, 2020.

described how Gubbio embodies the preferential option for the poor through relationships that privilege the perspective of the poorest.

> And so, what religion asks of us, I think in its sort of New Testament way, is to give to the poorest because they need it most and to be among them and to be part of that community with them. It's something I've sort of been thinking about a lot in the last few months, and then I've brought up at several meetings because we talk about our values at Gubbio quite a bit. . . . There's this idea of sort of reducing yourself down to being on the lowest level and to understand what is happening in these communities that are so negatively affected. Of course, this is all coming from an atheist, so I could be completely wrong.[21]

This self-described atheist captures a theological concept that is central to the Christian faith—self-emptying love or *kenosis*. He goes on to describe the importance of sharing a meal with guests.[22] While some volunteers and staff do not eat the meal they serve to the guests, he regards it as an essential practice. The difference between being in community with others and "communing" with them lies in one's willingness to move beyond barriers of understanding, to sleep on the mats, to eat what they are eating. Again, he describes the self-emptying humility required for this Gospel-centered way of relating to others.

The concept of *kenosis* is central to understanding what Richard Kearney describes as the sacramental moment of the "anatheistic wager."[23] Kearney's 2010 book *Anatheism: Returning to God after God* offers one way to grasp spirituality and ethics in a post-secular context.[24] The existence of God cannot be taken for granted, evoking

21. Interview with Gubbio participant on April 3, 2020.

22. The original site for Gubbio, where I did my fieldwork, does not serve meals but the second site offers weekly breakfast.

23. Richard Kearney, *Anatheism: Returning to God after God* (New York: Columbia University Press, 2010).

24. I use the concept post-secular in the way Taylor employs the concept of secular, namely, that there are multiple ways of relating to faith, ranging from a full embrace of religion to a rejection of religion.

epistemological humility. It is possible, Kearney argues, to return to belief in God after the twentieth-century masters of suspicion,[25] but it is not the God of omnipotence. The anatheistic wager refers to a choice in this context, to embrace God as the stranger with hospitality over hostility. This stance is translated concretely into an openness toward other religions and a commitment to hospitality toward the stranger, the refugee, the person experiencing homelessness. Kearney describes:

> Here again, I would argue, we encounter the anatheist choice between hospitality and hostility. A wager that we witness daily as one part of humanity strives for more dominion, while another opts for sacramental care of the non-sovereign stranger. This is not part of some dialectical destiny, but a decision for each one. The Yes or No to the estranged in our midst. The opening or closing of the door to uninvited guests.[26]

The woman who anointed the feet of an unhoused guest at Gubbio manifests the sacramental praxis that Kearney describes. Her yes to the stranger speaks to the sacred in a way that does not deny the secular. Those who observed her expression of radical hospitality toward the other experienced the sacred in a visible, tangible way. Kearney recognizes this experience of the sacred in everyday life as sacramental: "The sacramental moment of anatheism is when we finally restore the hyphen between the sacred and the secular."[27]

Kearney lifts up Dorothy Day as one who breaks down the dualism of sacred and secular that makes the anatheistic stance possible.[28] Dorothy Day illustrates Kearney's notion of sacramental praxis in ways that are particularly relevant to Gubbio. First, inspired by the Gospel,

---

25. This refers to three post-Enlightenment thinkers, Karl Marx, Sigmund Freud, and Frederick Nietzsche, who not only questioned the existence of God but, in different ways, exposed how religion could be used ideologically to control, suppress, or alienate people.

26. Kearney, *Anatheism*, 160.

27. Kearney, *Anatheism*, 153.

28. Kearney, *Anatheism*, 163.

Day dedicated her life to an incarnational solidarity with the impoverished and unhoused. The Catholic Worker is synonymous with radical hospitality and nonjudgmental, low-barrier openness to all. Second, Day, like many people I spoke to, had a complex relationship with the church. Although she was a devout Catholic, she lived in "permanent dissatisfaction with the church,"[29] always expecting more from Catholic leaders in light of the demands of the Gospel. The third reason I focus on Day is that she signals the relationship between beauty and justice.

Day, baptized in the Episcopal church, grew up without a strong relationship to organized religion. However, in her diaries she talks about a deep knowledge of God connected to her sensitivity to beauty. She spent much of her childhood near the water, in New York and San Francisco, and named the beach as the place "where so many years ago the beauty of creation plunged me into the faith, entranced me."[30] She also describes feeling drawn to the beauty of Catholicism before and after her conversion—the stained-glass windows, rosaries, statues, and incense. Her love of the sacraments reflected this embodied spirituality, one that appealed to all the senses.

Her conversion toward the poor preceded her conversion to Catholicism. In her autobiography, *The Long Loneliness*, she recalls walking through the meatpacking district of Chicago after reading Upton Sinclair's *The Jungle* had left her sensitized to the suffering of impoverished immigrants laboring in the factories. She saw the people living and working there. She saw their suffering, striving, and longing for a better life. And in this encounter, she felt a profound connection to them. She writes, "from then on my life was to be linked to theirs; their interests were to be mine; I had received a call, a vocation, a direction to my life."[31]

Catholicism would eventually nourish this vocation but only after she encountered its radical edges. Day was distrustful of organized

---

29. Dorothy Day, *The Long Loneliness* (San Francisco: Harper & Row, 1981, first published in 1952).

30. Dorothy Day, *Duty of Delight: The Diaries of Dorothy Day*, ed. Robert Ellsberg (Milwaukee: Marquette University Press, 2008), 583.

31. Day, *Long Loneliness*, 38.

religion, seeing the hypocrisy of religious leaders who failed to embody the values they professed. As a young journalist and activist, she surrounded herself with Marxists and bohemians who matched her desire for revolutionary social change and restlessness with the state of the world. But Day's longing for community that had been awakened in her conversion toward the poor drew her to the Catholic Church as well. She came to see how much the church meant to the poor immigrants she desired to know and love. And she encountered individuals in the church who lived authentically the radical commitment to the poor that drove her own sense of purpose. Ultimately, she decided to join the Catholic Church after the birth of her daughter, an experience marked by an enlarged capacity to love and a desire for her child to have a sense of community and stability.[32]

Her relationship with radical French peasant and intellectual Peter Maurin gave vision and language to her personalist approach to solidarity and her spirituality rooted in the Gospel. Maurin envisioned an alternative society transformed by person-to-person encounters inspired by a literal reading of the Beatitudes. His Gospel-centered vision met Day's action-oriented sense of vocation, and they started the Catholic Worker newspaper and houses of hospitality. The effectiveness of the newspaper, aimed at consciousness-raising, depended on the concrete relationships with people experiencing poverty and homelessness.

In her diaries, Day wrote about Maurin's vision, which she embraced as her own. "By the practice of voluntary poverty, he says. If you give what you have, with no thought for the morrow, the Lord will constantly multiply the loaves and fishes for you. And we were to live in beauty as the birds of the air and the lilies of the field."[33] For Day, it was the experience of freedom in community that had been missing in her previous life. In her autobiography, she reflected, "I have been passing through some years of fret and strife, beauty and ugliness, days and even weeks of sadness and despair, but seldom has there been the quiet beauty and happiness I have now. I thought all those years I had

32. Day, *Long Loneliness*.
33. Day, *Duty of Delight*, 493.

freedom, but now I feel that I had neither real freedom nor even a sense of freedom."[34]

Ultimately, Day's restlessness and longing for community was satisfied in her relationship with God. And her relationship with God was sustained by ongoing encounters with Christ in the Eucharist and by her relationship with the poor. Through an incarnational spirituality, Day saw herself as a guest in God's presence in the Eucharist and with the poor. So, when she welcomed impoverished and unhoused guests into her home, she experienced herself as host and guest at the same time.

Day's commitment was sustained not only by the sacraments but also by her lifelong love of literature. Her diaries are filled with references to Dostoevsky and in particular a quote from *The Idiot*, "The world will be saved by beauty." She often evoked this quote without elaboration, usually in response to violence or injustice. It was clear from her writings that she understood beauty to be a reflection of God that could be grasped. Beauty is love made visible, which offers a possibility for faith beyond belief in God. "What is more beautiful than love? . . . For those who do not believe in God—they believe in love."[35]

Gubbio attests to the redemptive quality of beauty. Staff and volunteers frequently refer to the beauty of the church—not only the church space but the practices that occur in the space. The beauty is presented as a contrast to the reality outside the walls of the church. The visibility of street homelessness, a defining characteristic of San Francisco, is encountered in an embodied way. Consistently, staff and volunteers describe the Tenderloin as an assault to the senses—the noise and smells, the images of people lying on the streets, people denied basic necessities. Entering the church touches the person on an equally visceral level—the sounds of snoring, the smell of incense and feet, the images of people resting in safety, in a pew of their own.

Describing the contrast of his home outside of San Francisco, one volunteer explained, "I would drive into the city, and I would just see bodies, you know, they're people, they're people that are lying there.

---

34. Day, *Long Loneliness*.
35. Day, *Long Loneliness*, 294.

People on the street like, you know, it's, it's just very visible in San Francisco. The poverty is very visible."[36] This volunteer offered a similarly embodied description of the encounter that drew him to Gubbio:

> So then the Tenderloin was featured [in an article] and specifically Gubbio, and there's that amazing shot that they take from where the organ sits and the balcony face down. You can see all the bodies, all the folks sleeping and getting their rest. And it just conjured up imagery of similar folks being in similar situations, having to share a common space . . . whether they're down on their luck or they're trying to improve their lives for an opportunity. It just felt like something I wanted to be a part of.[37]

I regularly observed this longing at Gubbio. Even among those who have been wounded by the church and those who are thoroughly disenchanted with religion, there is a lingering desire to see the embodiment of the Gospel. The beauty of Gubbio is redemptive because it transforms relationships wounded by the violence of street homelessness. Day knew intuitively the connection between beauty and justice, and she was able to find beauty everywhere, even in the ugliness of human suffering. To better understand the relationship between suffering, beauty, and justice, I will turn to another woman who rejected religious institutions but like Day, loved God, Christ, and the sacraments—Simone Weil.

Beauty and Suffering

> I was just incredibly drawn to the beauty and the peace within the church. It was a very visceral moving experience. I remember walking in with our group and just feeling something and that feeling really did stick with me. . . . In normal times, I go every Wednesday for my lunch break and actually, it's at this really interesting time of the week because it's the middle of the week. It's kind of this focal point and I feel like I am always walking away more grounded and just with this enhanced perspective on life

---

36. Interview with Gubbio participant on April 6, 2020.
37. Interview with Gubbio participant on April 6, 2020.

because I'm able to connect with these beautiful people in ways that I wouldn't be able to connect with them otherwise.[38]

The young woman quoted above describes the role of beauty in drawing her to Gubbio and shifting her relationship with unhoused people in San Francisco. Her story provides a rich context for reflection on spirituality, beauty, and justice. She describes herself as nonreligious. Unlike many of the volunteers, her story did not involve personal wounds from religion. It was simply absent from her upbringing. She describes a cultural connection to Buddhism that formed a sense of her spirituality, but she distinguished this from organized religion. She admits having a negative perception of religion because too often she sees religious institutions promoting exclusion, judgement, and hate. Gubbio represents a contrast experience. It is not clear to me if she associates Gubbio with Christianity. She approaches the religious symbolism in the place with curiosity. Volunteering at the supply closet, she hands out socks and hygiene kits. Occasionally, guests will ask for a rosary or Bible. She speculates on the importance of these items and of religion more generally in providing resilience for the guests to cope with their suffering.

She stumbled upon Gubbio while participating on a popular tour of the Tenderloin by a well-known resident leader and activist. She described walking into the church and seeing the beauty of the place, which evoked an experience in her that made her want to volunteer. But what drew her to the Tenderloin in the first place is also worth noting. She spoke about the enormity of the problem of homelessness in San Francisco. Like many people I interviewed, she struggles to come to terms with this prominent characteristic of a city she loves and enjoys. She experiences guilt over her privilege, working for a tech company and benefiting from an economy that affords this industry many benefits. She recognizes the role of tech companies in gentrifying the city she loves, adding to her discomfort over the economic inequality.

Moreover, she cites concrete experiences of walking by homeless people on the streets that ignite a sense of injustice. She pays attention

---

38. Interview with Gubbio participant on April 8, 2020.

to her own response to the image of street homelessness. She laments looking away, avoiding eye contact, feeling something diminished within herself when she ignores or walks away from their suffering. Volunteering with Gubbio has been redemptive for her. She not only connects with unhoused people during her shift, but she leaves with an "enlarged perspective" that allows her to encounter and interact with people on the streets differently, in a way that affirms their humanity and enacts her own beliefs and values.

I am struck by the way she evokes beauty—not only as that which drew her to Gubbio but also in her description of the people at Gubbio. The space is beautiful and the people with whom she connects are beautiful. This experience of beauty, in this case, is not simply a matter of pleasure or aesthetic sensibility. In fact, the church is messy and run down, with scratches on the pews and the smell of feet only partially masked by incense. The people are run down from living on the streets with dirty clothes and body odor. The experience of beauty is situated in the context of suffering and vulnerability. Furthermore, it is transformative, generating an "enlarged perspective" that goes beyond the immediate experience.

Simone Weil, a French thinker and activist born to an agnostic Jewish family in 1909, articulated a compelling experience of beauty in suffering which related to her mystical experience of God and sense of justice. Weil, like many people I interviewed, rejected religious institutions but was drawn to Christianity because she regarded it as "preeminently the religion of slaves."[39] Weil uses the metaphors of slavery and death to describe affliction—extreme psychological, physical, and spiritual suffering. She arrived at this understanding of affliction when she plunged herself into the reality of 1930's factory workers and saw unrelenting physical labor and poverty.[40] Weil's dramatic commitment

---

39. Simone Weil, *Waiting for God*, trans. Emma Craufurd, Routledge Rivals Edition (London: Routledge, 2009, first published in 1951), 14.

40. John Hellman, *Simone Weil: An Introduction to Her Thought* (Waterloo, ON: Wilfrid Laurier University Press, 1983).

to solidarity with those who experience affliction was the basis of her unconventional spirituality.

She writes on the relationship of beauty and mysticism:

> The beauty of the world is the mouth of a labyrinth. The unwary individual who on entering takes a few steps is soon unable to find the opening. Worn out with nothing to eat or drink, in the dark, separated from his dear ones, and from everything he loves and is accustomed to, he walks on without knowing anything or hoping anything, incapable of discovering whether he is really going forward or merely turning round on the same spot. But this affliction is as nothing compared with the danger threatening him. For if he does not lose courage, if he goes on walking, it is absolutely certain that he will finally arrive at the center of the labyrinth. And there God is waiting to eat him. Later he will go out again, but he will be changed, he will have become different, after being eaten and digested by God. Afterward he will stay near the entrance so that he can gently push all those who come near into the opening.[41]

According to Weil, the experience of affliction creates a decentering of self that allows union with God, described in dramatic mystical language here, likened to being consumed by the Divine. Weil had a taste of this mystical union with God through the experience of beauty, which she described in a letter to a priest and friend. Weil had an experience in a Romanesque chapel in Assisi, where St. Francis used to pray, that "compelled me for the first time in my life to go down on my knees,"[42] though it did not convert her to Christianity. She experienced a decentering of self through beauty that created a space to connect to the Divine through attention—to desire without trying to dominate or consume, to let the other be other. Like St. Francis of Assisi, whom Weil deeply admired, she connected her mystical experience to a self-emptying solidarity with the poor.

---

41. Weil, *Waiting for God*, 60.
42. Weil, *Waiting for God*, 14.

The decentering experience of beauty prepares a person to behold the suffering of another. "None of our efforts to turn our attention wholly on something other than ourselves is ever wasted. Should the occasion arise, they can one day make us better able to give someone in affliction exactly the help required to save him, at the supreme moment of his need."[43] It is through attention, a focused receptivity, that one is able to love another as they are, beyond one's own desires and beyond utility. Similarly, Hannah Arendt describes the role of beauty in allowing us to behold the other as an end in itself.[44] From this perspective, the experience of beauty provides a foundation for a society that resists the instrumentalization of persons. Weil's insistence on the connection between beauty, spirituality, suffering, and justice provides a helpful starting point for an analysis of what makes Gubbio a sanctuary space.

Beauty and Justice

Philosopher Elaine Scarry elaborates on the connection between beauty and justice. She makes her case in a post-metaphysical context, wherein it cannot be assumed that beauty points to the transcendent. A classical notion of beauty, following Plato, emphasizes its objective, ideal qualities. Until Immanuel Kant reflected on the subject's experience of beauty, philosophical and theological aesthetics pointed beyond this world. Beauty, for Augustine and Aquinas, originated in God and pointed the beholder back to God. This cannot be assumed in a secular context, where the belief in God is not taken for granted.

Scarry argues that beauty still has a place in the discovery of what is good and true and just without reference to God. She writes:

> Because the sky is equally distributed throughout the world—because its beautiful events are equally distributed—it will not be surprising if the population in large numbers, or even unanimously, agree that the beautiful sky should continue. Because

43. Weil, *Waiting for God*, 36.
44. Sara MacDonald, "Simone Weil and Hannah Arendt on the Beautiful and the Just," *The European Legacy* 24, no.7/8 (2019): 805–18.

most of its manifestations—its habit of alternating between blue and black, the phases of the moon, the sunrise and sunset—are present everywhere, those voting do not need to know where they are living to know that they will be beneficiaries.[45]

Here Scarry points to the vast beauty of the sky to argue that beauty is inherently distributive. It exists for everyone. She develops this by pointing to the qualities of beauty that mirror John Rawls's distributive justice. Beauty is encountered in symmetries, revealing to us a quality of justice in relationships. Beauty promotes ongoing regeneration, touching upon the human desire to create. Scarry connects this to Rawls's notion of duty to bring about just social conditions, in addition to supporting those that exist.[46]

The quote above reveals another important aspect of Scarry's argument. The beauty of the sky evokes a desire to care for it, to protect it, and to see it continue. Some might argue that contemplating the beauty of the sky poses a distraction from things we don't want to face, like poverty and violence. However, Scarry rejects the idea that beautiful things distract us from other worthy concerns. Setting things apart as "precious" and worthy of protection does not take away from the principle of fairness. It is through the experience of beauty in particular objects that we develop the capacity to care beyond our immediate interests.[47]

Scarry picks up on Weil's insight that beauty prompts a decentering that allows a person to assume a posture of attention. Building on Weil, as well as Iris Murdoch's notion of "unselfing," Scarry argues that beauty disrupts asymmetries of power and promotes inclusive participation and fairness.[48] So the experience of the beauty of the sky, the sense that it belongs to everyone and is worthy of care, does not remain with that experience. It gives rise to our ability to create justice. Scarry states that "beautiful things give rise to the notion of distribution, to a lifesaving

45. Elaine Scarry, *On Beauty and Being Just* (Princeton: Princeton University Press, 2001), 120.

46. Scarry, *On Beauty*, 115.

47. Scarry, *On Beauty*.

48. Scarry, *On Beauty*.

reciprocity, to fairness not just in the sense of loveliness of aspect but in the sense of a symmetry of everyone's relation to one another."[49]

When I asked staff and volunteers if being in a church space made a difference at Gubbio, many observed that people tend to respect the church space. Only two people I interviewed talked about the fear that guests would destroy the beauty or "desecrate" the space, but no one reported observing this behavior. The integrity of the space and the religious art has remained for everyone to enjoy, perhaps confirming Scarry and Weil's insight that we want to care for precious things.

The beauty of Gubbio is not a distraction from the suffering on the streets. As Weil describes, beauty evokes attention toward reality. It allows us to see affliction without looking away, avoiding eye contact, or hurrying past someone lying on the street. Going back to Dorothy Day's incarnational spirituality is illuminating here. The bodies of unhoused guests finding respite in the pews are sacramental, in the sense that they reveal a God whose radical self-emptying allowed God to become a homeless refugee, a friend of the outcast who overcame violence with love. Those who are drawn into this sacramental experience participate in the transformation of relationships through solidarity. Conceiving sanctuary as sacramental praxis has implications for ecclesiology. To conclude this chapter, I will identify some preliminary insights on the theology of the church as sacrament made visible through the praxis of solidarity.

An Ecclesiology of Sacramental Praxis

In her reflection on what allows the church to speak with public credibility, Mary Hines points to the sacramental, incarnational view of the church lifted up at Vatican II.[50] The image of the church as the Body of Christ developed in *Lumen Gentium* makes explicit the connection between the embodied reality of the church and its effectiveness in

49. Scarry, *On Beauty*, 42.

50. Mary Hines, "Ecclesiology for a Public Church: The United States Context," *Proceedings of the Catholic Society of America* 55 (2000): 23–46, at 25.

witnessing to the Gospel. The 1979 Synod of Bishops' "Justice in the World," made this point explicitly: "While the Church is bound to give witness to justice, she recognizes that anyone who ventures to speak to people about justice must first be just in their eyes. Hence we must undertake an examination of the modes of acting and of the possessions and lifestyle found within the Church herself."[51] This is particularly important in a secular context that does not assume the authority of the church. In a context marked by multiple experiences of faith, including negative experiences, the church's actions speak more loudly than words. Pope Francis emphasizes this in his understanding of evangelization as attractive witness.[52] Stan Chu Ilo describes Francis's theology of the church as "illuminative ecclesiology" centered on a "form of witnessing and proclamation that can be experienced as a transformative encounter with the Lord Jesus Christ by all—Christians and non-Christians— through the priorities and practices of the church."[53]

Pope Francis reinforces this vision in his desire for a "church which is poor and for the poor."[54] In *Evangelii Gaudium*, Francis challenges the church and individuals to examine their own lifestyles, recognizing the idolatrous power of consumerism to undermine the common good. Rooted in the Gospel, Francis presents the preferential option for the poor as a mark of authenticity of the church, "We may not always be able to reflect adequately the beauty of the Gospel, but there is one sign which we should never lack: the option for those who are least, those whom society discards."[55] This requires a dedicated praxis of solidarity, which Francis differentiates from episodic moments of generosity. Solidarity points to habitual actions that transform unjust structures and ultimately restore to the poor what is theirs by virtue of the universal destination of created goods.[56]

---

51. Synod of Bishops, *Justice in the World* (Washington, DC: USCCB, 1972), 44.
52. EG, 14.
53. Ilo, *A Poor and Merciful Church,* 29.
54. EG, 198.
55. EG, 195.
56. EG, 189–90.

Francis demonstrates the meaning of solidarity in his 2020 encyclical, *Fratelli Tutti*, by inviting the reader into the story of the Good Samaritan. He describes the social conditions that create barriers to solidarity, allowing us to "look away" when we encounter suffering:

> Let us admit that, for all the progress we have made, we are still "illiterate" when it comes to accompanying, caring for and supporting the most frail and vulnerable members of our developed societies. We have become accustomed to looking the other way, passing by, ignoring situations until they affect us directly. . . . What is more, caught up as we are with our own needs, the sight of a person who is suffering disturbs us. It makes us uneasy, since we have no time to waste on other people's problems. These are symptoms of an unhealthy society. A society that seeks prosperity but turns its back on suffering.[57]

Francis speaks directly to the volunteers and staff of Gubbio who describe the disturbing experience of "looking away" before ongoing encounters transformed their relationships with unhoused people. Through the story of the Good Samaritan, Francis points to the primacy of praxis over religious affiliation. Religious exemplars were among those who looked away from the suffering man, demonstrating that "belief in God and the worship of God are not enough to ensure that we are actually living in a way pleasing to God." In fact, Francis notes, "those who claim to be unbelievers can sometimes put God's will into practice better than believers."[58] The mark of an "authentic openness to God"[59] is openness toward others, particularly the stranger or the excluded with whom Christ identified. Francis quotes the Gospel, "I was a stranger and you welcomed me" (Matt 25:35), to reinforce an incarnational theology that locates the encounter with God through relationships with "abandoned or excluded brothers and sisters."[60]

---

57. FT, 64–65.
58. FT, 74.
59. FT, 74.
60. FT, 85.

Francis's ecclesiology reflects a foundational conviction in liberation theology; namely, the primacy of right action (orthopraxis) over right teaching (orthodoxy). Gustavo Gutierrez highlighted the primacy of praxis when he described theology as a second act, following and inextricably linked to the lived expression of Christianity in history.[61] Because Gutierrez regards salvation history not as "otherworldly" but connected to human history, he locates Christian praxis in "the struggle for a just society."[62] This understanding of salvation as liberation of the oppressed frames Gutierrez's sacramental ecclesiology:

> As a sacramental community, the Church should signify in its own internal structure the salvation whose fulfillment it announces. Its organization ought to serve this task. As a sign of the liberation of humankind and history, the Church itself in its concrete existence ought to be a place of liberation. A sign should be clear and understandable . . . [and] since the Church is not an end in itself, it finds its meaning in its capacity to signify the reality in function of which it exists.[63]

Shawn Copeland also locates the praxis of solidarity at the center of what it means to be church. She lists barriers to solidarity, including selfishness and apathy toward oppressive dehumanization. Solidarity as compassionate action involves *kenosis*: "Self-dispossession (kenosis) calls for critique of autonomy as will-to-power, of obscurant individualism, of irresponsibility; but, we must go further, deeper, beyond the boundaries of our lives/ourselves to a new way of being in the universe, in God's future."[64] For Copeland, solidarity is always embodied.

---

61. Gustavo Gutierrez, *A Theology of Liberation,* 15th Anniversary Edition with a New Introduction by the author, trans. Caridad Inda and John Eagleson (Maryknoll, NY: Orbis, 1988).

62. Gutierrez, *A Theology of Liberation,* 168.

63. Gutierrez, *A Theology of Liberation,* 147.

64. M. Shawn Copeland, *Knowing Christ Crucified: The Witness of African American Religious Experience* (Maryknoll, NY: Orbis, 2018), 146.

Copeland offers a rich incarnational theology of the church that emphasizes Jesus's embodiment. As the flesh of Jesus, the church is called to stand at the feet of those who are crucified in history—those who suffer social oppression because of race, gender, sexuality. "The body of Jesus of Nazareth impels us to place the bodies of the victims of history at the center of our theology. His love calls us to break bonds imposed by imperial design, to imagine and grasp and realize ourselves as his own flesh, as the body of Christ."[65] As the flesh of Jesus, the church also reflects all aspects of embodiment—sexuality, race, gender. When the church excludes people because of racism and homophobia, it fails to model the embodied solidarity it professes. "The sacramental aesthetics of Eucharist, the thankful living manifestation of God's image through particularly marked flesh, demands the vigorous display of difference in race and culture and tongue, gender and sex and sexuality."[66]

Gutierrez and Copeland help us understand how seeing the dehumanizing suffering on the streets transformed in an embodied way at Gubbio is sacramental. It not only signifies God's radical incarnational love for humanity but evokes participation though the praxis of solidarity. The transformation of relationships between housed and unhoused people, the deepening of mutuality, is central to this practice of sanctuary. In the next chapter, I will explore how the decentering experience of beauty and the transformation of relationship in the space allow a thirdspace to emerge. This space, constructed by rituals that reinforce the material nature of the space as church also resist it, making it a home-space, a refuge for the unhoused.

65. Copeland, *Knowing Christ Crucified*, 80.
66. Copeland, *Knowing Christ Crucified*, 78.

Chapter 5

Sanctuary as Radical Hospitality

itting in the front of the church looking toward the back, I see rows of pews, all occupied. Most people sleep, some lie awake, looking at the church ceiling or at their phone. For those who do not have a pew of one's own, there are a number of spaces on the floor in the back. It is still delineated as personal space by their possessions—blankets, clothes, shoes, and bags. I am told that regular guests who prefer the back tend to go to the same space each morning.

Today, I watch a young African American woman in a pew toward the front. She does not sleep, though she appears to be quiet and calm. I watch her carefully organize her possessions. She methodically folds her clothes and separates them into bags of various sizes that she has brought with her. I am struck by the intimacy of this moment and suddenly feel self-conscious as an observer.

The night before, I sat in silence, folding my family's laundry, placing them into neatly organized piles. This mundane task is not simply something I perform in the privacy of my home, it is one way I *create* home. Once I started paying attention not only to rituals that reinforce the space as a church but also those rituals that speak to the space as a home, I began to see the complexity of Gubbio as a sanctuary.

When describing what makes Gubbio special, a number of staff and volunteers pointed to the presence of women, indicating to them that the space is experienced as safe. Homelessness among women and children is less visible on the streets, but here they can see women resting, unafraid of harassment or assault. The sense of safety that marks Gubbio as a refuge is not created by the presence of strict rules or powerful authorities to enforce them. We have explored the importance of being in a physical church space, one marked by beauty and a sense of the sacred, but the material reality of the church is only one aspect of it.

In between the church created by Franciscan brothers that operates as a Catholic parish in the Tenderloin and the church/nonchurch that allows an interfaith practice of radical hospitality with unhoused people, there is another space. The practices I observed at Gubbio—dipping into the holy water, gestures of prayer, looking up at one's cell phone before falling asleep, putting on slippers and shuffling to the bathroom, sorting clothes and putting them into bags, whispering to a partner—cannot be neatly categorized. Rituals of church and rituals of home exist in the same space, contesting the categories of public versus private, sacred versus profane.

The physical space matters; our shared interpretations of it matter. And Gubbio reveals another space, where meaning is constructed and contested; where it is both church and nonchurch, home-space and public space. There is another space between the material aspects of space—the "churchy" sights and smells one perceives upon entering—and the interpretive aspects of space—the mental associations that give the space meaning and evoke memories of church when one walks in the door. Sanctuary emerges in this relational, situational space. Conceiving of sanctuary in this way contributes to a growing body of thought among theologians who, responding to the spatial turn in philosophy, have emphasized sacred space as constructed, contested, and embedded in practice.

Political geographer Edward Soja, along with postcolonial and feminist thinkers, have used the notion of "thirdspace" to describe the reality in between the material space we perceive and analyze (i.e., the physical church building) and the interpreted space we conceive and imagine (the meaning associated with church space). Thirdspace overcomes a binary approach to time and space as it recognizes that space is constantly being constructed and reconstructed through relationships, intersectional identities, and struggles for recognition and belonging. As an in-between reality, thirdspace is marked by the possibility for reimagination, resistance, and transformation.[1]

Thirdspace takes seriously the social construction of space in a way that resists the separation of time and space. Spaces shape action and the actors shape and reshape space through social practices.[2] Therefore, spaces and spatial practices are sites of power, resistance, and social justice. Soja, following Michel Foucault and Henri Lefebvre, insists that people are spatial as much as we are temporal and social. This spatial turn in philosophy has influenced theological conceptions of space and ritual, opening up possibilities for reconceptualizing sacred space and sanctuary practice. This section will draw upon this body of literature to explore how Gubbio is a refuge, constructed through rituals of home and rituals of church, breaking down rigid boundaries between sacred and secular, private and public.

When these categories are made fluid by ritual practices, the conditions for radical hospitality are possible. Radical hospitality, a feature of field hospital ecclesiology, is marked by relationships of mutuality. Rather than fixed roles as guest or host, radical hospitality is achieved when barriers to mutuality are overcame through accompaniment.

Constructing Home-Space

A Church but not a Church

The church opens up its doors and transitions from being a traditional church to a space where those experiencing homelessness can come and get uninterrupted sleep because it's so challenging

---

1. Homi Bhabha, *The Location of Culture* (London: Routledge, 1994); Edward Soja, *Thirdspace: Journeys to Los Angeles and Other Real-and-Imagined Places* (Cambridge: Blackwell, 1996); and bell hooks, *Yearning: Race, Gender, and Cultural Politics* (Boston: South End Press, 1990). See also *Thirdspace: A Journal of Feminist Theory & Culture*.

2. Doreen Massey does not use the language of thirdspace but describes a union of time and space in her conception of space as a process ("Philosophy and Politics of Spatiality: Some Considerations: The Hettner-Lecture in Human Geography," *Geographische Zeitschrift* 87, no. 1 [1999]: 1–12).

to get uninterrupted sleep when you're living on the streets. And so Gubbio provides that safe space, no questions asked, and it is really a sanctuary.[3]

Responding to the question, "How would you describe Gubbio to a friend?" this volunteer suggests a transformation from being a traditional church to a place of sanctuary. The physical space does not change, but the doors are opened, literally and metaphorically, and sanctuary emerges. This question prompted a variety of responses that spoke to the space as a church and nonchurch. Sometimes the churchyness of Gubbio is emphasized through the beauty inscribed in the Romanesque architecture, the history of the space, the religious symbolism and art. Sometimes the difference was highlighted. Churches are exclusionary, Gubbio is open; churches are rule-bound, Gubbio functions with very few rules. So the safety of the place is connected to both its reality as church and nonchurch. Sanctuary emerges in the in-between tension, relating to both, but distinctive.

Sanctuary has been associated with liminality,[4] a term used by anthropologist Victor Turner to describe the "betwixt and between" experience of identity in periods of transition.[5] Turner uses the concept to describe rites of passage, which temporarily suspend typically structured social life in order to transition to a different phase of social life. Social structures are held in a dialectical relationship with the immediate unstructured experience of *communitas*.[6] In this nonstructured period, roles and hierarchies are suspended, opening possibilities for reimagination. Turner draws upon various examples, including an initiation rite in Zambia to the emergence of hippie culture in North

---

3. Interview with Gubbio participant on April 10, 2020.

4. Hilary Cunningham, *God and Caesar at the Rio Grande: Sanctuary and the Politics of Religion* (Minneapolis: University of Minnesota Press, 1995).

5. Victor Turner, *The Ritual Process: Structure and Anti-Structure* (London: Routledge, 2017, first published in 1969): 94–130.

6. Turner uses the Latin term *communitas* instead of the English translation "community" to differentiate the concept from typical usage of "an area of common living" and emphasize it as a "modality of social living" (*Ritual Process*, 96).

America, to describe the role of this dialectic in maintaining social life as a balance of law and openness, authority and revolution.[7]

This captures the phenomenon of sanctuary as something set apart that allows for a reassignment of relationships. It offers a temporary suspension of normality. But the concept of liminality is generally associated with a period of time, whether a rite of passage or social movement, marked by a transition that suspends normality. To understand sanctuary in this case, one needs to embrace the spatial, in addition to and as equally important as the temporal.

Michel Foucault's *heterotopia* is related to liminality but one that is thoroughly connected to space. Like liminal spaces, heterotopia represents rites of passage. Foucault points to the honeymoon location, the cemetery, the vacation village. They function to suspend time, but unlike utopias, they represent an actual physical space. Like public spaces, they are sites of negotiation, but unlike public spaces, they do not claim to be neutral. In this sense, they are fixed and open at the same time, as Gubbio is a church and nonchurch simultaneously. Heterotopias have the "curious property of being in relation with all the other sites, but in such a way as to suspect, neutralize, or invert the set of relations that they happen to designate, mirror, or reflect. These spaces, as it were, . . . are linked with all the others, which however contradict all the other sites."[8] Foucault names two types of heterotopias that function in this way. Heterotopias of illusion expose aspects of real space that often go unnoticed, and heterotopias of compensation create a space set apart from the messiness of real spaces.[9] Thinking specifically of Gubbio as a heterotopia allows us to grasp the way sanctuary emerges as a paradox, reinforcing and resisting the church as a church. The experience of sanctuary created at Gubbio is inseparable from the church space, but there is a noticeable shift in what the space becomes through the practices that make Gubbio what it is—the rituals of hospitality, the delineation of personal space, and so forth.

7. Turner, *Ritual Process*.

8. Michel Foucault, "Of Other Spaces," *Diacritics* 16, no. 1 (Spring 1986): 22–27, at 24.

9. Foucault, "Of Other Spaces."

The heterotopia is a heuristic concept that enables a spatial analysis beyond the material and ideological aspects of space. This thirdspace suggested by Foucault was developed at length by French Marxist philosopher Henri Lefebvre. Space, for Lefebvre, is not neutral but actively shaping and reflecting goals of social life. His spatial analysis points to three ways space functions: spaces of representation (how space is conceived), spatial practice (how space is perceived and used), and representational space (how space is lived). Lefebvre's triad corresponds with mental, physical, and social dimensions of space.[10]

As a Marxist, Lefebvre is interested in the way material spaces carry ideology, exercising power through the way they are conceived. Speaking specifically of religious representations of space, he states:

> What is an ideology without a space to which it refers, a space which it describes, whose vocabulary and links it makes use of, and whose code it embodies? What would remain of a religious ideology—the Judeo-Christian one, say—if it were not based on places and their names: church, confessional, altar, sanctuary, tabernacle? What would remain of the Church if there were no churches? The Christian ideology, carrier of a recognizable if disregarded Judaism . . . has created the spaces which guarantee that it endures.[11]

Spatial practices can reinforce or contest dominant conceptions of space. This second dimension of Lefebvre's triad speaks to lived, taken-for-granted knowledge that is embedded in the way people interact with space. While spaces of representation speak to the reified, ideological dimension of space, spatial practices speak to the cultural, symbolic, interpretive dimensions of space that usually exist in the background of human interaction.

Considering these dynamics in the context of Gubbio, one can see more clearly how knowledge and power are transmitted through the

---

10. Henri Lefebvre, *The Production of Space*, trans. Donald Nicholson-Smith (Oxford: Blackwell, 1991, first published in 1974).

11. Lefebvre, *Production of Space*, 44.

space as a church. The Franciscan brothers who designed the space inscribed their beliefs and priorities into it. The Romanesque structure communicates the grandeur of God, the sacredness of the space as set apart from the world outside. The walls and stained-glass windows depict biblical stories, highlighting the history of salvation and the centrality of Christ. The focal point of the space is the altar, where the authority of the priest is reinforced in the administration of the sacraments.

Some spatial practices reinforce this conception of space as a conveyor of power and knowledge. These include obvious practices during the celebration of the mass—the gestures and language particular to roles of priest and laity, Christian and non-Christian, are expressed during the liturgy. Religious ritual relies on embodied knowledge that is often unconscious and automatic, communicating a sense of what the space is about. When people walk in the door of Gubbio, they habitually dip their fingers into the holy water. They lower their voices. They perform the sign of the cross. The lived knowledge communicated in these practices does not necessarily imply technical knowledge of Christianity built into the architecture of the space. Spatial practices at Gubbio also resist the representations of space as a church. Rituals of home—sleeping, bed-making, folding laundry, getting dressed—defy dominant notions of church, breaking down boundaries of public-private; sacred-secular.

Lefebvre's third category, representational spaces, are related to the material (perceived) and interpreted (conceived) aspects of space, but they are distinctively related to the social imagination of a community. This is a particularly dynamic space where meaning is constructed through an interaction of culture, biography, and embodied practice. "Representational space is alive: it speaks."[12] Representational space engages the affect. As examples, Lefebvre names the bedroom, home, church, and graveyard.[13] As a distinctively symbolic, social space, representational spaces can be sites of resistance and reimagining.

---

12. Lefebvre, *Production of Space*, 42.
13. Lefebvre, *Production of Space*, 42.

Edward Soja picks up on the thirdspace thinking in Lefebvre and Foucault. Soja argues that the thirdspace between the material and interpreted creates possibilities for communities to exercise agency to resist hegemony and oppression. By emphasizing the social aspect of space, these thinkers overcome the preference for the temporal in Western thought and demonstrate a dynamic interplay of social, temporal, and spatial dimensions of human activity:

> In this way, our lives are always engaged in what I have described as a socio-spatial dialectic, with social processes shaping spatiality at the same time spatiality shapes social processes. Stated another way, our spatiality, sociality, and historicality are mutually constitutive, with no one inherently privileged a priori.[14]

This spatial consciousness allows Soja to overcome what he describes as a disembodied Rawlsian account of justice that pervades Western thought. He puts forth an approach to justice that takes seriously the way geographies give rise to and are shaped by injustices, such as the exploitation of workers and oppressive structures, such as racism and sexism. Focusing on examples from Los Angeles, he examines movements against gentrification and environmental racism.[15] For Soja, as for many feminist and postcolonial thinkers, thirdspace represents possibilities for resisting dominant narratives, for recognizing hybridity and difference, and for mobilizing praxis.

bell hooks describes this space of resistance in her development of homeplace. Through autobiography, hooks reflects on how Black women create spaces of refuge from white supremacy through fostering a nurturing home environment. hooks acknowledges the sexist and racist history that relegated Black women to this role. Domestic work is reinforced by an essentialist view of women as naturally suited for the housework and childrearing and is situated in a racist history of Black women's servitude in the homes of white families. Yet hooks recognizes

14. Edward Soja, *Seeking Spatial Justice* (Minneapolis: University of Minnesota Press, 2010), 18.

15. Soja, *Seeking Spatial Justice*.

homeplace as a site of resistance, subverting the dominant meaning of home and gender. It does not deny the suffering and injustice Black women face, but it also does not deny the way they resist oppression.[16]

This concrete example illustrates hooks's insistence of marginality as a site of resistance. She develops this concept through her story of journeying from rural poverty into academia and refusing to be an "exotic other" in the dominant discourse on marginalization. Those who embody and remember a "lived experience" of marginalization offer a disruptive presence. hooks writes, "I am located in the margin. I make a definite distinction between that marginality which is imposed by oppressive structures and that marginality one chooses as site of resistance—as location of radical openness and possibility."[17]

Conceiving Gubbio as a thirdspace helps us understand the significance of space in the practice of sanctuary. The space is a refuge because of the social space imagined and lived out in the church. The *decentering* of relationships that happen in the space attest to the instability and multiplicity of meaning. Resisting oppressive exclusion, guests become hosts by enacting rituals of home and establishing a space for one's self and possessions. Volunteers and staff become ministers in cultivating the beauty and safety of the space. In this way, the safety is generated—not by rules or threats of force but out of the relationships themselves. Attesting to the social dimension of space, these relationships shape the space and are also shaped by it.

Constructing Sacred Space

Kim Knott, who has integrated Lefebvrian spatial theory into a theology of space, suggests, "Whilst space cannot be said to exhibit agency itself, it affects agency in those who experience and participate in space."[18] Space, for Knott, is not simply the background of social life

---

16. bell hooks, "Homeplace: A Site of Resistance," in *Yearning*, 41–49.

17. bell hooks, "Choosing the Margin as a Space of Radical Openness," *Framework: The Journal of Cinema and Media*, no. 36 (1989): 15–23.

18. Kim Knott, *The Location of Religion: A Spatial Analysis* (London: Routledge, 2005), 129.

but exists in a dynamic relationship with it. Her theology emphasizes how space is produced and reproduced through practices. Space, religious or secular, is constructed. "There is nothing intrinsically religious or secular about spatial practice. Religious meaning or purpose may be attributed to it; it may acquire a sense of sacrality from being enacted in a religiously meaningful space or may be transformed by ritual process."[19]

Knott embraces a social constructivist approach to space, which allows her to recognize the significance of sacred space in a postmetaphysical context. Following geographer Lily Kong and scholars of religion David Chidester and Edward Linenthal, Knott organizes discourse on sacred space in two categories: a phenomenological approach focused on the "poetics" of space and a social constructivist approach focused on the "politics" of space. The political approach, which sees spaces and bodies as sites of power, discourse, and contestation, emerges more recently in theology and religious studies, following the spatial turn represented by Foucault, Lefebvre, and Michel De Certeau. It allows Kong and Knott to consider the experience of the sacred beyond official religion.

Mircea Eliade represents the phenomenological[20] approach concerned with the poetics of sacred space. Eliade offers a substantive distinction between the sacred and profane, where the sacred "irrupts" as an experience of the "real" or an experience of "power."[21] Similarly, Rudolf Otto describes the experience of the "holy" as one that interrupts ordinary experience.[22] Sacred spaces, then, are set apart from the ordinary by what they reveal and the orientation they provide. This reality is distinguished from the profane, which is neutral, lacking a

---

19. Knott, *Location of Religion*, 39.

20. This fits within Knott's categories; however, Belden Lane locates Eliade among ontological approaches to space, distinguishing this from cultural approaches to space represented by Chidester and Linenthal. See Belden C. Lane, "Giving Voice to Place: Three Models for Understanding American Sacred Space," *Religion and American Culture* 11, no. 1 (Winter 2001): 53–81, at 57.

21. Mircea Eliade, *The Sacred and the Profane* (New York: Harper & Row), 1961.

22. Rudolf Otto, *The Idea of the Holy*, trans John W. Harley (London: Oxford University Press, 1950).

particular center or orientation. Belden Lane follows Eliade's phenomenological approach to the extent that he assumes sacred "spaces are
not chosen but revealed."[23] Lane's thought provides a good example
of what Kong and Knott describe as the poetics of sacred space, as he
describes his experience of the sacred in nature, marked by "a deep
sense of being connected in a single moment to everything present."[24]

Chidester and Linenthal differentiate the substantial approaches
of Eliade, Otto, and Lane from situational approaches that recognize
sacred space as socially constructed. Following Jonathan Z. Smith,[25]
they reinterpret Eliade by arguing that sacred space is set apart—not
by an essential difference between the sacred and profane but through
embodied human practices that are always entangled in layers of
knowledge, meaning, and power. Exemplifying the politics of space
because of their highly symbolic and interpreted quality, Chidester and
Lilienthal argue that sacred spaces, even more than ordinary spaces,
are sites of contestation:

> Sacred places are arenas in which power relations can be rein-
> forced, in which relations between insiders and outsiders, rulers
> and subjects, elders and juniors, males and females, and so on,
> can be adjudicated. But those power relations are always resisted.
> Sacred places are always highly charged sites for contested ne-
> gotiations over the ownership of the symbolic capital (or sym-
> bolic real estate) that signifies power relations.[26]

Considering Gubbio in this framework allows us to consider the
significance of sacred space in sanctuary in a way that is relevant and
credible in a post-secular context. Sanctuary represents a place set apart,
but not through an ontological category of the sacred. Rather, it is

23. Belden C. Lane, *Landscapes of the Sacred: Geography and Narrative in American Spirituality* (Mahwah, NJ: Paulist Press, 1988).

24. Lane, "Giving Voice to Place," 55.

25. Jonathan Z. Smith, *Map is Not Territory: Studies in the History of Religions* (Chicago: University of Chicago Press, 1993, first published in 1978), 88–103.

26. David Chidester and Edward T. Linenthal, *American Sacred Space* (Blooming-ton, IN: Indiana University Press, 1995), 16.

ritually produced through bodies in a particular space. Space matters as a site of contestation—a thirdspace where meaning is negotiated outside predetermined categories of public-private, sacred-profane. The sacred emerges as a powerful embodiment of the central Christian narratives that disrupt social hierarchies. Unhoused people are not guests in the church. They are at home in a double sense—by reclaiming a right to a space of one's own that is denied on the outside, and they are at home because, at its most authentic, Christianity is a religion for the impoverished and oppressed.

Rituals of Home, Rituals of Church

Understanding sanctuary as a constructive interaction of space and practice departs from notions of sanctuary as mythically dependent on sacred spaces or sanctuary as a political movement that can be divorced from space. This shift toward a social constructivist understanding of sanctuary provides the context for arguing that the recipients of sanctuary are active agents in its construction. They do not "receive" sanctuary by those who hold ecclesial and political power.

Following Foucault's insight on power as embedded in social relationships, one can see how sanctuary is a dynamic negotiation of power. Gubbio becomes a refuge when unhoused people enter the doors and delineate their own home-space within the church. But the church remains a church, ensured not only by the Franciscan brothers who minister in the space and celebrate the sacraments. Housed and unhoused guests at Gubbio perform rituals to reinforce the space as a church. Boundaries are reinforced and challenged at the same time. Guests "know" not to enter the holiest space around the altar. They "know" that a pew is someone's bed when they see their possessions delineating personal space.

This knowledge is embodied knowledge, an expression of one's personal history of church and home that is always situated within the cultural meaning assigned to these categories. The embodied knowledge is expressed and reproduced in embodied practices, reflecting a sense of what church and home mean. These expectations, made concrete and visible through practices such as dipping one's hand in holy water, give rise to the reality of Gubbio in the present and future.

This observation relates to Pierre Bourdieu's complex and central concept of *habitus*. Bourdieu develops the concept to reflect the interaction of objective and subjective aspects that construct social life. It reflects the assumption that people are shaped by social structures and their experiences of them in history. But people are not passive products of socialization. They are also agents of social life, constructing the meaning and processes that continually act upon them. On the concept of *habitus*, Bourdieu writes, "It expresses first the result of an organizing action, with a meaning close to that of words such as structure; it also designates a way of being, a habitual state (especially of the body) and, in particular, a predisposition, tendency, propensity, or inclination."[27]

Applying Bourdieu's thought to religious ritual, Catherine Bell demonstrates how ritual does not simply reflect meaning but strategically produces it. The strategic aspect of action is important to Bell's understanding of ritual activity. Without rejecting Emile Durkheim's basic suggestion that religion functions to create social cohesion, Bell challenges the idea that ritual should be interpreted solely as a means of social control. Ritual practices include a strategic dimension that allows people to "reproduce or reconfigure a vision of the order of power in the world," a process Bell describes as "redemptive hegemony."[28]

Bell's understanding of ritual as strategic practices to disrupt and reconfigure power relationships is dependent on Foucault's insights on power. Foucault challenges a prevalent notion of power as dominion, which misses the way power is "always a way of acting upon an acting subject or acting subjects by virtue of their acting or being capable of action."[29] Following Foucault, Bell assumes that power is always functioning in the context of relationships and is therefore, situational, fluid, and local.

---

27. Pierre Bourdieu, *Outline of a Theory of Practice* (Cambridge: Cambridge University Press, 1977), 214.

28. Catherine Bell, *Ritual Theory, Ritual Practice* (Oxford: Oxford University Press, 1992), 81.

29. Michel Foucault, "The Subject and Power," in *Michel Foucault: Beyond Structuralism and Hermeneutics*, 2nd ed., ed. Hubert L. Dreyfus and Paul Rabinow (Chicago: University of Chicago Press, 1983), 220–22. Quoted in Bell, *Ritual Theory*, 200.

Based on this understanding of power, Bell points out that participation in ritual always involves consent. At first glance, rituals appear to be controlling as actors unconsciously reproduce taken for granted knowledge that maintains social cohesion. But when one considers how one participates in the enactment of knowledge and power through ritual, this interpretation seems simplistic. Bell points out that some rituals may seem disempowering but are actually acts of resistance because "Ritualization, as the interaction of the social body with a structured and structuring environment, specifically affords the opportunity for consent and resistance and negotiated appropriation on a variety of levels."[30] Reinforcing this point, Bell highlights how US Catholics appropriate and subvert papal authority at the same time. She notes the ritualistic enthusiasm they displayed when John Paul II came to the United States, implying devotion to the papacy. This is juxtaposed with the fact that many US Catholics disagree with John Paul II's pronounced papal teaching on birth control. Again, ritual practice is not only a means of social control; participation allows for resistance.[31]

Bell's approach to ritual is particularly helpful in naming the reality of power asymmetries embedded in social practices, as well as the ways people exercise subjectivity within a hegemonic power structure. These practices are redemptive in the sense that they "facilitate the envisioning of personal empowerment through activity in the perceived system."[32] So the hierarchical structure and dogmatic exclusivism associated with the church is real, but this reality is not experienced in the same way by all people. Furthermore, hierarchies can be disrupted and contested through practices that may or may not be observable to an outsider.

Applying Bell's insights to Gubbio helps us understand how unhoused guests exercise agency in producing the church/nonchurch space. When someone enters the church to sleep, dips their fingers in the holy water and makes the sign of the cross, they are not only

30. Bell, *Ritual Theory*, 209.
31. Bell, *Ritual Theory*, 214.
32. Bell, *Ritual Theory*, 84.

performing the expectations that delineate church space, they are also contesting the boundaries by reinterpreting what a church is for. Entering the church to sleep, ritualizing home through making a bed, and arranging one's possessions challenges the knowledge, power, and boundaries of the church.

Home, like church, exercises its own hegemony, which is also contested through spatial practices at Gubbio. Although home has been conceived as a safe haven or sanctuary, it has also been a space of domination or violence. Anthropologist Mary Douglas has observed that home is not a building or fixed location, but a space brought under control.[33] Following this understanding of home as a cultural category allows us to explore it as space where power is negotiated. Feminist thinkers have pointed out how cultural and religious assumptions that associate women with domesticity are reinforced by a gendered distinction between the private and public sphere. The resulting exclusion of women from the public sphere has historically denied them political and economic power.

This dualism has been difficult to overcome, despite the feminist movement. Nancy Fraser and others have argued that capitalism relies on a romanticized notion of home as a refuge from the public sphere of competition. Associating the domestic sphere with essentialist notions of women as nurturing and self-sacrificing reinforces a gendered social order. Capitalism, Fraser argues, relies on the free domestic labor that women assume in this structure.[34]

The resulting cultural romanization of the home has not only excluded women from the public sphere, but it has also rendered domestic concerns as private or dangerously invisible. Julie Tobler has challenged the uncritical assertion that the home is experienced as a sanctuary for women, referring specifically to domestic violence and

33. Mary Douglas, "The Idea of Home: A Kind of Space," in *The Domestic Space Reader*, ed. Chiara Briganti and Kathy Mezei (Toronto: University of Toronto Press, 2012), 51.

34. Nancy Fraser, "Contradictions of Capital and Care," *New Left Review* 100 (July/August 2016): 99–117.

the prevalence of sexual assault of women in the home. Tobler argues that the home is a political space, a site for the negotiation of power.[35]

Home, like the streets, can be a dangerous place, especially for people who do not fit into the dominant model of the heteronormative, patriarchal family structure. In her study of unhoused women, sociologist Julie Wardaugh observes, "Those who are not able, or choose not to, conform to the gender, class, and sexuality ideals inherent in establishing a conventional household, find themselves symbolically (and often literally) excluded from any notion or semblance of home."[36] This analysis can be expanded to include those who are gender nonconforming. Women and LGBTQ people experiencing homelessness are also more vulnerable to the dangers of street life. The safety they experience at Gubbio, as a church and home space, is doubly redemptive.

Some feminist thinkers have emphasized the ways women exercise agency in the creation and maintenance of the home. bell hooks's homeplace as a space of resistance and refuge from the violence of white supremacy offers a powerful example.[37] Iris Marion Young also wants to retrieve the domestic space and values associated with it in a way that empowers women as preservers of memory and identity, which cannot be commodified. She argues that "the idea of home and the practices of home-making support personal and collective identity in a more fluid and material sense, and that recognizing this value entails also recognizing the creative value of the often unnoticed work that many women do."[38]

These theories highlight the ambivalence of home. Considering these insights in light of Bell's notion of redemptive hegemony, one can see the rituals of home performed at Gubbio as assertions of agency that create alternative experiences of home among unhoused people.

---

35. Judy Tobler, ' "Home is Where the Heart Is?': Gendered Sacred Space in South Africa,'" *Journal for the Study of Religion* 13, no. 1/2 (2000): 69–98.

36. Julie Wardaugh, "The Unaccommodated Woman: Home, Homelessness and Identity," *Sociological Review* 47, no. 1 (1999): 92.

37. hooks, "Homeplace."

38. Iris Marion Young, "House and Home: Feminist Variations on a Theme," in Briganti and Mezai, *Domestic Space Reader*, 193.

Those for whom home has been oppressive or exclusionary find a home space at Gubbio. In this sense, Gubbio is a home sanctuary and church sanctuary, redeeming both ambivalent categories through the agency of those who have been disempowered or excluded.

Gubbio is a sanctuary, characterized as a place of safety and refuge, because of a dynamic interaction between the physical space, the interpretations of the space, and the practices that generate an alternative space that is both church and home. Acknowledging that space is socially constructed in no way undermines the significance of sacred space in sanctuary. Rather, it fosters a theology that recognizes the agency of those seeking sanctuary. More than discovering sanctuary, those who seek sanctuary participate in creating it. Sanctuary, in this sense, is marked by a transformation of relationships, where those who have been disempowered and excluded are cocreators of a different experience. In this case, it is marked by beauty, belonging, and safety.

The ecclesiological and ethical implications of this understanding of sanctuary are significant beyond the context explored here. Although I focus specifically on the expression of sanctuary to those who are unhoused, the ecclesiology that demands an authentic praxis of liberation carries significance beyond this concrete manifestation. A mark of the church as a field hospital is one that disrupts injustice by embodying God's liberating action through radical hospitality.

An Ecclesiology of Radical Hospitality

Sanctuary for me is so deeply entwined with radical hospitality and radical welcome. At Gubbio, really being as barrier-free as possible, and welcoming people however they are, whoever they are, whatever their experience is, or the choices they've made, or the circumstances they've found themselves in, that's the radical hospitality piece. You are welcomed in all of who you are into this sacred space to be as you need to be. That, to me, is so core to sanctuary, and so core to who Gubbio is and aspires to be.[39]

39. Interview with Gubbio participant on March 24, 2020.

Sanctuary at Gubbio reveals a church marked by radical hospitality. Hospitality was not the most commonly evoked term to describe Gubbio. And yet the themes summarized in this quote by a staff member speak to what ethicists and theologians have retrieved and named as a central quality of the church: radical hospitality marked by mutually transformative relationships and a low-barrier, nonjudgmental welcome. Guests and hosts mutually create the sacredness of the space. Radical hospitality offers a prophetic alternative to the idea of private property, particularly the neoliberal view of private property as unlimited, individual, and absolute. It makes concrete Pope Francis's field hospital ecclesiology, which is porous and mobile so it can accompany people in their suffering and meet them where they are.

This expression of sanctuary also resists misconceptions of Christian hospitality that lack mutual transformation rooted in authentic encounter and shared risk. This dominant understanding of hospitality, informed by the experience of welcoming a guest into one's home, does not capture what happens in the thirdspace of sanctuary, a likely reason why hospitality rarely came up in conversations or interviews. The church space as constructed at Gubbio belongs to no one, not even the church. Radical hospitality at Gubbio subverts hierarchically structured relationships among housed and unhoused people, creating the possibility for mutual transformation.

Barriers to Mutuality

In her work on Christian ethics and homelessness, Laura Stivers points to the prevalence of charity over solidarity among Christian responses, "Church members might venture out and volunteer . . . but how many churches have opened their sanctuary doors to people who are homeless?"[40] She argues that benevolent responses to homelessness reflect the same erroneous cultural perception as those who view unhoused people with disdain. Viewing the homeless person as the "diseased other," one tries to avoid them or promote policies that

---

40. Laura Stivers, *Disrupting Homelessness: Alternative Christian Approaches* (Minneapolis: Fortress Press, 2011), 124.

push them out of sight. There is a parallel narrative that relies on the image of the homeless person as mentally ill, addicted, or just "down on their luck," which promotes treatment for the "diseased other." Stivers points to research that illustrates while mental illness and addiction are prevalent among many unhoused people, many people do not suffer in these ways. The single common cause of homelessness in this country is oppressive poverty. And focusing on individual illness or bad luck does not address the economic structures that perpetuate severe inequality.[41]

Drawing upon ethicist Traci West, Stivers argues for an ethic of disruption to address homelessness. This involves an analysis of structures that perpetuate homelessness and an honest reflection on the perceptions and practices that maintain the oppressive status quo. Christians need to create a prophetic social movement to address homelessness rather than focus on charity. In this way, Stivers radicalizes the concept of Christian hospitality by connecting it to liberating praxis that empowers unhoused people to have a seat at the table. She points out: "Jesus challenged those who tried to limit the seats at the banquet table and offer crumbs rather than abundant loaves. Hospitality as charity does not afford the recipients full human dignity in ways that enable them to participate fully in community and fellowship."[42]

Christine Pohl traces the history of hospitality in Christianity to recover its prophetic dimension. She points out that early Christian practices of hospitality were shaped by Christians' own experiences of marginality and identity of being a persecuted community. The marginality of the host is reinforced by three biblical themes: "the relation between alien status and covenant, Jesus as guest and host, and Christians as aliens yet members of God's household."[43] When Christians were no longer persecuted, the monastic tradition reenacted

41. Stivers, *Disrupting Homelessness*.

42. Stivers, *Disrupting Homelessness*, 126.

43. Christine Pohl, "Hospitality from the Edge: The Significance of Marginality in the Practice of Welcome," *The Annual of the Society of Christian Ethics* 15 (1995): 121–36, at 125.

this communal practice of hospitality that was still perceived to be a central act of the church.

Today, hospitality is generally perceived to be an individual act, informed by an experience of welcoming people into one's home, not an ecclesial act that transcends property ownership. Pohl argues that "As Christians became more well-established in positions of influence and wealth, their marginal status was lost and their hospitality increasingly reflected and reinforced social distinctions rather than transforming or transcending social differences."[44] Pohl points out that throughout Christian history, private property has been moderated by a theology and related social ethic that recognizes the universal destination of goods. When interpreted through the lens of stewardship, Kelly Johnson argues, this teaching resists the disruptive ethic that Stivers recommends. Johnson contrasts the rational ethic of the steward with the radical approach of St. Francis and Peter Maurin, for whom begging was an enactment of marginality.[45]

Although radical hospitality is part of Christian theology and practice in history, there are significant barriers to the experience of mutuality and shared marginality. When hospitality is perceived to be an individual act, the ecclesial dimensions are obscured. If hospitality is conceived as a sharing of one's property, even when tempered by a theology of stewardship, the power of the host is reinforced. It is clear that the neoliberal economy and state work together as a significant barrier to radical hospitality. William Cavanaugh has argued that when the state's role is the protection of private property, it "becomes one of the primary promoters of homelessness." In this context, he argues that Christians need to "tell a more profound story" that disrupts the unquestioned logic of liberalism.[46]

---

44. Pohl, "Hospitality from the Edge," 130.

45. Kelly Johnson, *The Fear of Beggars: Stewardship and Poverty in Christian Ethics*, Eerdmans Ekklesia Series (Grand Rapids: Eerdmans, 2007).

46. William Cavanaugh, "Strategies from Below: Subsidiarity and Homelessness," in *Street Homelessness and Catholic Theological Ethics*, ed. James Keenan and Mark McGreevy (Maryknoll, NY: Orbis, 2019), 148.

Hospitality as Accompaniment

Cavanaugh makes a strong case for spaces like Gubbio, arguing for alternative spaces that suspend barriers to mutuality between housed and unhoused people:

> More than a distribution of money, we need a distribution of people living in community, finding ways of living that bring vulnerable and less vulnerable people together. The church cannot simply leave the care of the homeless to the state but needs to create spaces that pull people with property out of their comfort zones and put them into contact with the chaos of others.[47]

Similarly, in *Fratelli Tutti* Pope Francis lifts up people who "identify with the vulnerability of others" as exemplars of solidarity.[48]

Similarly, Kate Ward has emphasized the importance of encounter in her virtue-based social ethic. Ward also challenges notions of hospitality that fail to transform power asymmetries embedded in social structures. Echoing Pope Francis, she also emphasizes the importance of shared vulnerability, "Reclaiming a view of hospitality as a risky virtue allows us to pursue a practice of hospitality that refuses to prioritize an idolatrous view of our own safety over others' basic justice."[49] Ward's view is informed by the social teaching of Pope Francis, who similarly uses the language of idolatry to describe neoliberalism as a barrier to solidarity.

Pope Francis emphasizes the primacy of encounter in breaking down the barriers to mutuality. He has argued for the kinds of alternative spaces that Cavanaugh envisions, where housed and unhoused, refugee and citizen, wealthy and poor meet face to face and share life together. Ward suggests that Francis's approach to hospitality reflects his Jesuit identity. While we tend to associate hospitality with monastic traditions, particularly Benedictines, for whom hospitality is a central

47. Cavanaugh, "Strategies from Below," 154.

48. FT, 67.

49. Kate Ward, "Jesuit and Feminist Hospitality: Pope Francis' Virtue Response to Inequality," *Religions* 8, no. 4 (2017): 6.

charism, the Jesuits have developed an approach to hospitality that flows from their outward orientation. Following James Keenan, Ward describes hospitality in the Jesuit tradition as one of accompaniment—one that "goes out and meets people on the road where they are."[50]

Through accompaniment or walking with the other, both people move beyond their comfort zones so that mutual transformation can occur. Reflecting on their experience walking with unhoused people, Mary Scullion and Christopher Williams, a formerly unhoused person, offer this insight:

> In true accompaniment, both persons are changed. As we get to know men, women, and children who experience poverty and homelessness, we begin to recognize the distorted ways our society values persons based on their success and productivity, or the way human dignity is often bound up with material accomplishments and belongings. Poverty forces us to strip that veil away. Poverty makes us confront the stark truth that suffering is a universal and inescapable part of being human and that we cannot be fully human until we embrace the truth of suffering.[51]

Sanctuary as radical hospitality reveals a dimension of Pope Francis's field hospital church. The church as a field hospital, through accompaniment, breaks down separations of sacred and secular, host and guest. It provides that alternative space to contest an instrumentalist view of the person created to serve the goals of capitalism. Gubbio embodies radical hospitality because it decenters relationships among housed and unhoused so transformative encounters can take place. Unhoused people are themselves the central agents in this decentering experience at Gubbio. By ritually constructing the space as church and home space, they create the sanctuary they seek.

50. Ward, "Jesuit and Feminist Hospitality," 7.

51. Mary Scullion and Christopher Williams, "Accompanying Each Other on the Journey Home," in Keenan and MacGreevy, *Street Homelessness*, 6.

Conclusion

began this project four years ago, as the United States prepared to inaugurate its forty-fifth president, Donald Trump. For some churches, along with other religious and nonreligious communities, the declaration of sanctuary represented an act of resistance to a particularly anti-immigrant political agenda. As I write this conclusion in January 2021, Donald Trump has been voted out of office and a number of his executive orders that targeted certain immigrant groups have been repealed or replaced. His successor Joseph Biden has promised to make it easier for migrants to seek asylum at the US-Mexico border. He has also proposed immediate protections for recipients of Temporary Protected Status (TPS) and Deferred Action for Childhood Arrivals (DACA) and a path to citizenship for immigrants in the United States who currently lack legal status.[1] A narrow definition of sanctuary, one defined by noninterference with federal immigration authorities, might be less urgent in this political moment.

---

1. See "Preserving and Fortifying Deferred Action for Childhood Arrivals (DACA)," January 20, 2021, at https://www.whitehouse.gov/briefing-room/presidential -actions/2021/01/20/preserving-and-fortifying-deferred-action-for-childhood-arrivals -daca/, and "Fact Sheet: President Biden Sends Immigration Bill to Congress as Part of His Commitment to Modernize our Immigration System," January 20, 2021, at https:// www.whitehouse.gov/briefing-room/statements-releases/2021/01/20/fact-sheet -president-biden-sends-immigration-bill-to-congress-as-part-of-his-commitment-to -modernize-our-immigration-system/.

However, sanctuary understood theologically as a *way of being church,* continues to be needed as long as humanity labors for the fullness of justice. Within the framework of Christian eschatology, sanctuary is a mark of the church situated in the "already" but "not yet" realization of God's liberating reign in history. Sanctuary as a concrete expression of the preferential option for the marginalized and vulnerable extends to migrants and refugees, the unhoused and impoverished, the ostracized and outcast. These experiences of marginalization due to nationality and economic inequality are intertwined and exacerbated by racism, sexism, and xenophobia.

The global COVID-19 pandemic has placed the dynamics of marginalization under a microscope. In this country, the highest rates of infection and death are among Black, indigenous, and Latinx communities. The Center for Disease Control and Prevention (CDC) connects these racial and ethnic health disparities to discrimination, economic inequality, and lack of access to healthcare. The CDC also explains that people of color are disproportionately represented in occupations that expose them to the virus—in factories, grocery stores, healthcare settings, and public transportation. Finally, some racial and ethnic minorities live in crowded multigenerational or multifamily housing due to cultural preference or economic necessity, making it difficult to practice social distancing.[2] A year into the pandemic, the discovery of effective vaccines has been a source of hope. Yet equity in distribution and access remains a top concern. In his Christmas 2020 message, Pope Francis called for cooperation, not competition or market logic, to guide the distribution of vaccines. He wants the most vulnerable to be first in line: "vaccines for all, especially for the most vulnerable and needy of all regions of the planet. Before all others: the most vulnerable and needy!"[3]

2. Center for Disease Control and Prevention (CDC), "Health Equity Considerations and Racial and Ethnic Minority Groups," July 24, 2020, at https://www.cdc.gov/coronavirus/2019-ncov/community/health-equity/race-ethnicity.html.

3. Pope Francis, "Urbi et Orbi" message for humanity (Christmas 2020), at http://www.vatican.va/content/francesco/en/messages/urbi/documents/papa-francesco_20201225_urbi-et-orbi-natale.html.

Sanctuary is needed in the midst of COVID-19 and in the years of recovery because those living on the peripheries have been further isolated by individualism and racism. In *Fratelli Tutti,* Francis calls for a transformation of social life to meet the challenges engendered by the pandemic. In the encyclical he rejects individualism, consumerism, and racism that undermine human dignity and solidarity. He articulates a robust vision of human rights, coupled with an expansive notion of community to argue for solidarity across borders. This explicit call to welcome migrants and refugees sets a clear path for the church. Additionally, Francis recognizes nongeographical peripheries that exist within communities because of racism and discrimination against people with disabilities. The same universal openness that implores us to break down borders challenges us to create more inclusive communities: "Every brother or sister in need, when abandoned or ignored by the society in which I live, becomes an existential foreigner, even though born in the same country."[4]

Solidarity, for Francis, is not abstract. Rather, it must be embodied concretely in actions. Writing on the connection between service and solidarity, Francis emphasizes closeness with the vulnerable, "Service always looks to their faces, touches their flesh, senses their closeness and even, in some cases, 'suffers' that closeness and tries to help them."[5] This person-centered immediacy of service, however, does not replace the long-term work of social change. Solidarity, Francis insists cannot be equated to "sporadic acts of generosity"[6] but involves transforming unjust structures at the heart of inequality and "confronting the destructive effects of the empire of money."[7]

Francis's statement points to the task of the field hospital church that he has consistently envisioned and enacted through embodied solidarity. It is a church on the peripheries, one situated in the messiness of the world, bruised and dirty from physical closeness to those

4. FT, 97.
5. FT, 115.
6. FT, 116.
7. FT, 116.

who are suffering. It is a community that holds space to welcome those who need refuge—"a home with open doors."[8] Sanctuary practices manifest this ecclesiology in visible and concrete ways through prophetic witness, embodied solidarity, sacramental praxis, and radical hospitality. This book explored these practices in a particular historical and geographical context—sanctuary among the undocumented and the unhoused of San Francisco. Yet sanctuary as a quality of the church extends beyond these particular manifestations. The theology of sanctuary constructed in this context has wider implications for ecclesiology, which I would like to summarize by way of conclusion.

Reimagining Religion and the Public Sphere

In January 2020, a group of women living in sanctuary partnered with the Austin Sanctuary Network and Free Migration Project to sue the federal government for violating their right to religious liberty. They allege that ICE targeted them as leaders in the sanctuary movement and charged them excessive fines for violating immigration law. Evoking the 1993 Religious Freedom Restoration Act (RFRA), they argued that embracing sanctuary is a concrete expression of their faith-convictions and offering sanctuary is an exercise of religious freedom.[9]

In 2019, Scott Warren, a humanitarian worker with the group No More Deaths, successfully defended his right to aid migrants on the US-Mexico border in federal court by similarly evoking religious liberty.[10] Yet the most prominent cases evoking the RFRA have been by

8. FT, 276.

9. Center for Constitutional Rights, "Women in Sanctuary File Lawsuit Against ICE to Challenge Retaliatory and Excessive Fines," January 19, 2020, at https://ccrjustice .org/home/press-center/press-releases/women-sanctuary-file-lawsuit-against-ice -challenge-retaliatory-and.

10. Elizabeth Reiner Platt, Katherine Franke, Kira Shepherd, and Lilia Hadjiivanova, "Whose Faith Matters? The Fight for Religious Liberty Beyond the Religious Right," Columbia Law School Law Rights and Religion Project, November 2019, at https:// lawrightsreligion.law.columbia.edu/content/whosefaithmatters.

individuals and for-profit companies around issues related to gender, family, and sexuality. Examples include the 2014 case in which Hobby Lobby, a for-profit company, successfully opposed the Affordable Care Act's mandate to provide health coverage for contraceptives to its employees at no cost. Another case involved a Colorado bakery owner who refused to provide services to a gay couple because he claimed that same-sex marriage violated his religious beliefs. Although a lower court found that the bakery violated the state's antidiscrimination law, the Supreme Court dismissed the case because they concluded that the hearing was not impartial with respect to his religious views.[11] Legal scholars have pointed out that it has been more difficult to win religious exemption cases for social justice issues such as economic justice, environmental justice, and immigration.[12]

Sanctuary churches have an opportunity in this moment to clarify the public role of faith in a way that goes beyond partisan politics or Christian exceptionalism. Conceiving sanctuary as prophetic witness provides a theological framework for understanding both *why* the church should be involved in social justice issues and *how* it should go about doing so in a pluralistic and secular context. Sanctuary practices exist across faith traditions and resonate with diverse theological and ethical visions. I hope that this exploration of the particularity of this ecclesiology will be part of a larger conversation on the role of faith in public life. This conversation, I have argued, cannot rely on rational translation, nor can it rely on religious exceptionalism or claims to exclusivity in a secular age. In a context marked by diverse approaches to faith, including the growing population of those who do not identify with a faith tradition, prophetic witness and praxis are essential.

Observing the way sanctuary churches perform their identities and core narratives in the public sphere confirms the critical role of public theology. Sanctuary is countercultural, not only as a defense

---

11. Laura Keeley, "Religious Liberty, Immigration Sanctuary, and Unintended Consequences for Reproductive and LGBTQ Rights," *Columbia Journal of Gender and Law* 37, no. 2 (February 19, 2018): 169–219.

12. Reiner Platt et al., "Whose Faith Matters?"

of solidarity beyond borders. Sanctuary in the Christian tradition resists the logic of unrestricted capitalism through space-sharing. In doing so, it disrupts the status quo by creating space for those who are excluded by political, economic, and social structures. This prophetic dimension of sanctuary can get lost in translation when limited to rational discourse. Sanctuary as noninterference with federal authorities represents an important aspect but incomplete picture of sanctuary when it is considered within a Christian theological tradition. Through the embodiment of one's core narratives through concrete practices, churches can continue to inform and disrupt the meaning of sanctuary.

Sanctuary practices likewise inform the identity of the church. For many churches, the declaration of sanctuary prompted a rereading of their own history or an announcement of a public identity. The declaration of sanctuary is most controversial among churches whose members disagree on the role of religion in politics. Yet, overwhelmingly, sanctuary practices reveal a church that is publicly engaged and resists the privatization of religion that is assumed within the Western liberal tradition. This points to an ecclesiology that emphasizes social engagement without compromising the interruptive power of the Gospel.

Pope Francis insists on the role of religion in public life because "An authentic faith—which is never comfortable or completely personal—always involves a deep desire to change the world."[13] Attentive to religious pluralism and nonreligious resources for social change, Francis emphasizes attractive witness over proselytization.[14] This is crucial in a secular age, marked by diverse ways of relating to faith. Because religious authority can no longer be taken for granted, churches must demonstrate their credibility through not only professing but embodying their beliefs.

Drawing upon Francis's field hospital ecclesiology informed by his social teaching, I have argued that sanctuary represents a concrete embodiment of the preferential option for the poor and marginalized. Therefore, sanctuary places the credibility of the church in the eyes of the marginalized. They are invited to judge whether or not the church

---

13. EG, 183.
14. EG, 14.

is a refuge for the excluded. This resonates with Francis's ecclesiology, which emphasizes accountability to the poor and vulnerable. He describes the poor as the evangelizers of the church.[15] Through ongoing encounter with the marginalized, the church becomes a sanctuary.

Key to my argument in this book has been that it is not enough to declare sanctuary on behalf of a church. A church community must be transformed by those seeking sanctuary through ongoing encounter. This process involves a decentering of relationships that are typically governed by asymmetries of power. A power analysis is needed in the discernment of sanctuary to discover and name the ways race, gender, class, and nationality show up in who decides and who does the work of sanctuary. This analysis, I argue, should inform the way a church conceives of and exercises its ministries. It echoes Pope Francis's call for pastoral closeness—leaders must be in relationship with the people they serve. In this case, those who represent the church's sanctuary commitment must be transformed through ongoing accompaniment of those seeking sanctuary.

Reimagining Sacred Space

The pandemic has highlighted the privilege of space and moral responsibility of a community to shelter the unhoused and vulnerable. In March of 2020, San Francisco scrambled to address a glaring weakness in the city's response to COVID-19. The mayor ordered everyone to shelter in place; yet over eight thousand people in San Francisco lack housing. Faith communities and housing advocates joined together to advocate for the city to house people in hotel rooms. California's governor explored creative options including housing people in vacant churches.[16]

Such urgency and creativity that inspired collective action in the midst of COVID-19 does not have to end with the pandemic if it is considered a concrete expression of the church's social mission.

15. EG, 198.
16. Kevin Fagan, "Coronavirus and Homelessness: SF wants to House People in Schools, Churches," *San Francisco Chronicle*, March 17, 2020, at https://www.sfchronicle.com/bayarea/article/Coronavirus-and-homeless-people-SF-wants-to-15138174.php.

Churches in San Francisco and other California cities have come together to address the state's housing crisis by examining how unused properties could be transformed into low-income housing and homeless shelters. Under the umbrella of a reappropriated acronym, YIGBY or "Yes in God's Backyard," churches are partnering with nonprofit organizations as well as city officials to navigate the complicated zoning and financing options to transform their properties in ways that align with their mission.[17] One San Francisco leader, Rev. Theresa Cho, who leads a Presbyterian sanctuary church, connects her work on affordable housing to the Gospel: "What are you to do as a church? You are to feed the hungry. You are to clothe the naked. Whatever is within that scope is within our mission. Affordable housing fits under that."[18]

Two of the churches highlighted in this book have discovered sanctuary as a concrete practice of sharing space with those who are unhoused. This ecclesial practice reclaims the spatial dimension of sanctuary and invites a deeper consideration of the nature of sacred space in a secular context. There is nothing magical about church space that makes it off-limits from ICE activity and the designation of "sensitive areas" relies on a cultural sensibility more than religious authority. Yet the practice of urban sanctuary among unhoused people highlighted in this book has demonstrated the power of sacred space in creating a refuge in the midst of homelessness and poverty.

My argument has relied on the assumption that in a secular or post-secular context there exists a longing for transcendence that expands traditional theological categories. Volunteers at Gubbio represent diverse ways of relating to faith including an explicit rejection of religion; yet there is an observable conviction that being in a church makes a difference in their experience relating to the people and space of Gubbio. The beauty of the space allows it to assume its own authority,

---

17. See the nonprofit organization, "Yes in God's Backyard," at https://yigby.org/.

18. J. K. Dineen, "Yes in God's Backyard: Bay Area's new answer to the housing crisis might be church property," *San Francisco Chronicle*, January 25, 2020, at https://www.sfchronicle.com/bayarea/article/Yes-in-God-s-Back-Yard-Bay-Area-s-new-answer-15002873.php.

freeing relationships at Gubbio from the power dynamics that typically govern religious institutions and homeless shelters.

Observing how the seekers of sanctuary interact with the space, ritually reinforcing and deconstructing the meaning of the space points to a constructivist notion of sacred space. Understanding the sacred beyond metaphysical categories allows us to embrace space set apart— not because of its unique nature but set apart through the way people interpret and interact with the space. I observe how sanctuary emerges in a thirdspace, beyond the limits of material space and dominant interpretations of it. What this means at Gubbio is that unhoused people construct the sanctuary they seek, transforming the space into a home and church, while strategically redeeming these categories that have themselves been sources of exclusion.

A spatial turn in theology has concrete implications on how we understand sanctuary and sacred space. Sanctuary is created in a dynamic interaction of time and space, expressed in material space as well as interpretations and spatial practices. The preference of time over space in theology has served to reinforce God's liberating action in history. For Pope Francis, time liberates while space consolidates power. Yet the category of thirdspace, seen concretely in sanctuary, opens possibilities beyond a dialectical understanding of time and space. Seekers of sanctuary disrupt the consolidation of power through spatial practices. This can be observed when a migrant offers their testimony during the Liturgy of the Word or an unhoused person delineates their own sleeping area in the worship space. The seekers of sanctuary create the refuge they seek. It is the role of the church to be transformed by those they accompany, which is possible through radical hospitality.

Reimagining the Church

The theology of sanctuary as espoused and practiced by Christian communities has given rise to a particular way of being church. It is rooted in historical practices of sanctuary—from the early church that welcomed criminals fleeing vengeance to an interfaith network of churches accompanying migrants and refugees. Conceiving contemporary practices broadly as a way the church cocreates a refuge for those marginalized by unjust structures, sanctuary gives rise to an ecclesiology rooted in the preferential option for the poor. This resonates in a particular way with the ecclesiology of Pope Francis. It fleshes out his field hospital church through concrete practices. At the same time, these ecclesial practices expand, augment, and challenge aspects of formal Catholic ecclesiology by highlighting the dynamism of the church as sanctuary.

By way of conclusion, I propose sanctuary to be a mark of the church alongside traditional ecclesiological categories—one, holy, catholic, and apostolic. Sanctuary manifests the church as a field hospital, one that is drawn to those who are suffering, called forth to the peripheries, one that meets people where they are and holds space for those who seek refuge. Theologically, sanctuary is a concrete embodiment of solidarity with the poor and vulnerable. This quality of the church illuminates other marks of the church as well. It serves as a hermeneutic to retrieve the meaning of these marks of the church in a contemporary, secular context.

Sanctuary is ecumenical, interfaith, and publicly engaged, highlighting the oneness or unity of the church beyond denominational and religious difference. Sanctuary engages and makes public the particularity of the Christian narrative, but it does so in a way that invites collaboration for a common purpose. Consider the image offered at the beginning of this book of religious leaders performing an interfaith celebration at a subway station. A celebration of Ash Wednesday, the ritual was saturated with Christian imagery but also meaningful across religious differences. Participating in an interfaith and public-facing expression of Christianity invites sanctuary churches to reread their own histories, making it a mutually transformative practice.

Sanctuary reveals the holiness of the church when it embodies its deepest convictions. Through praxis among those who suffer, it reveals God who became poor to be in solidarity with those who are marginalized. This is sacramental, revelatory beyond those who identify with Christianity but who seek justice and beauty and truth. This understanding of the church's holiness locates the church squarely in the world, engaged in the suffering of humanity, rather than set apart or self-contained. The holiness of the church is made visible when it is, as Pope Francis prefers, bruised and dirty from accompaniment.

Sanctuary represents the fullness of catholicity by pushing the church to be ever more inclusive and diverse. It manifests the global nature of the church by revealing the solidarity of humanity beyond borders. Inclusion extends beyond national borders to include borders set up in a single geographical location according to race, gender, sexuality, and experience of faith. Further, sanctuary challenges the church to manifest the unity in diversity it proclaims by decentering power dynamics to transform relationships within its structures.

Finally, sanctuary illuminates the apostolic nature of the church by calling forth all its members, lay and ordained, to actively proclaim the Gospel. The church proclaims the Gospel—not through proselytization but through prophetic witness, by embodying the transformative and liberating power of God's action in history. Pope Francis is clear about what this looks like. It is a poor church for the poor. Sanctuary represents a concrete way to become a poor church for the poor—by going to the peripheries and becoming a refuge to the excluded.

Index